Insight Text Guide

GM Dewis

Cat's Eye

Margaret Atwood

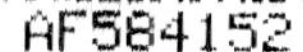

First published in 2011, reprinted 2011 by
Insight Publications Pty Ltd
ABN 57 005 102 983
89 Wellington Street
St Kilda VIC 3182
Australia
Tel: +61 3 9523 0044
Fax: +61 3 9523 2044
Email: books@insightpublications.com.au

www.insightpublications.com.au

National Library of Australia Cataloguing-in-Publication entry:
Dewis, G. M.
Margaret Atwood's cat's eye / G.M. Dewis.
9781921411922 (pbk.)
For secondary school age.
Atwood, Margaret, 1939–Cat's eye.
Atwood, Margaret, 1939–Criticism and interpretation.
813.54

Printed in Australia by Ligare

contents

CHARACTER MAP

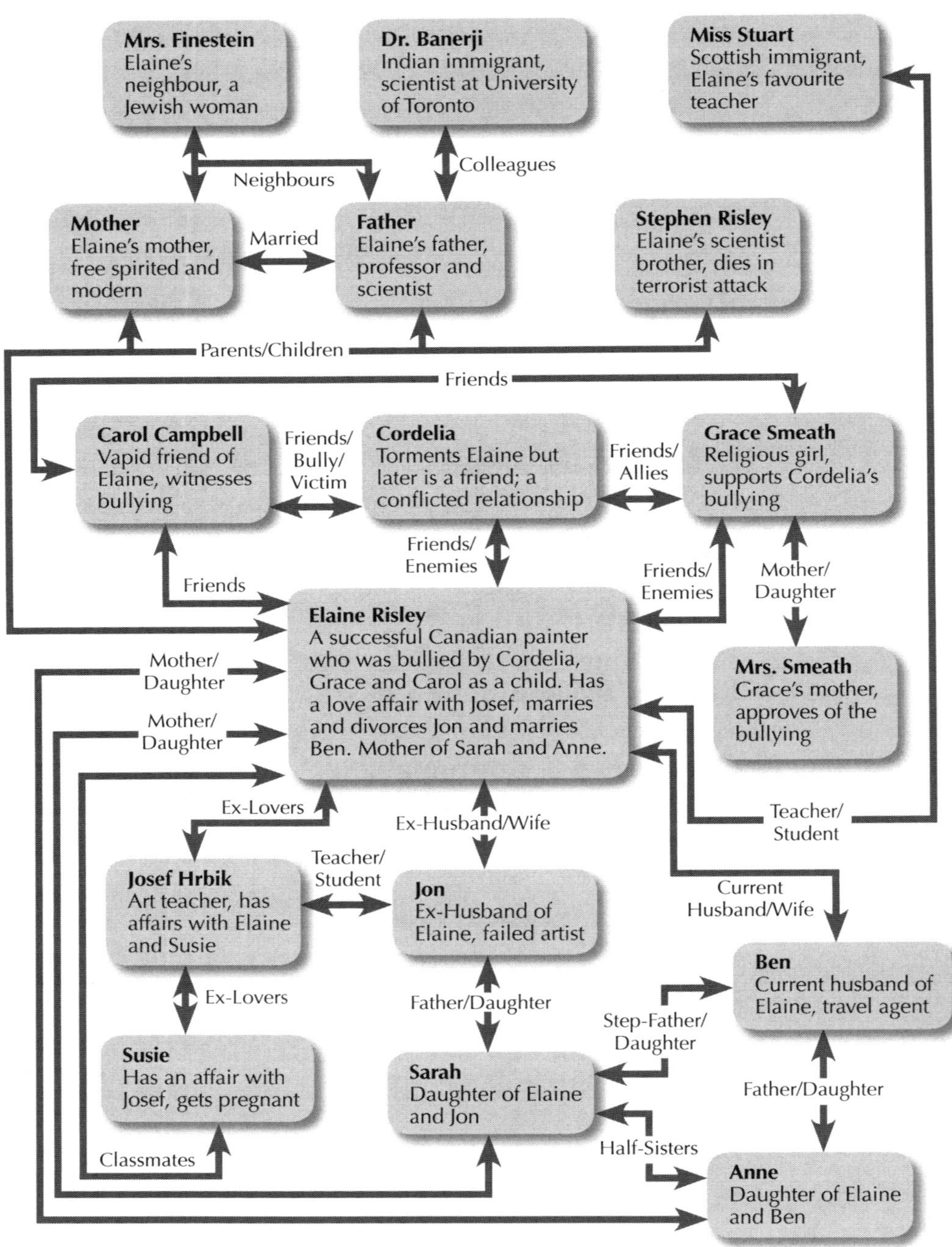

OVERVIEW

About the author

Margaret Atwood is considered to be one of the most successful Canadian writers alive today. The author of more than 40 books of fiction, poetry, children's literature and non-fiction, she is generally best known for her 1985 dystopian tale, *The Handmaid's Tale*.

Atwood's awards and honours are numerous, over eighty to date. They include the Governor General's Literary Award for Fiction (Canada), the Giller Prize (Canada), the Trillium Book Award (Canada), the Dan David Prize for Literature (Israel), the Los Angeles Times Fiction Award (USA), the Guggenheim Fellowship (USA), the Arthur C Clarke Award (UK) and the Booker Prize (UK). Atwood is one of only three Canadians to have won the prestigious Booker Prize, which she won for her novel *The Blind Assassin*.

She is also a well-known political and economics commentator. In Canada, she is generally considered to be associated with left-wing (liberal) politics, especially those of the environmental movement, and is a strong proponent of public funding for the arts. She and her partner Graeme Gibson (also a writer) are members of the Green Party of Canada. Atwood was born in Ottawa, Canada, in November 1939. Her father was an entomologist and she and her family spent many of the summers during her early life in the bush of North Quebec before moving to Toronto when she was seven. Toronto, where she currently lives, has provided the setting for many of her novels. She has lived in many cities in Canada, the USA and Europe.

In addition to fiction and poetry, Atwood has written several critical texts including *Survival: A Thematic Guide to Canadian Literature,* which is widely considered to be one of the most important and influential books ever written about Canadian literature. Atwood studied under respected Canadian literary theorist Northrop Frye at the University of Toronto and earned a Master of Arts degree at Radcliffe College, which later became part of Harvard University. Following her MA degree, Atwood began (though did not finish) a PhD at Harvard. She has taught at various universities and colleges and serves as a mentor for the masters degree in the field of creative writing program at her alma mater, the University of Toronto.

Atwood experienced literary success very early. By the time she was 30, in 1969, she had released her first novel, *The Edible Woman*, and five collections of poetry, the second of which won the prestigious Governor General's Literary Award in Canada. Since then she has remained a highly prolific writer in a number of different genres, even writing an opera libretto in 1964.

Synopsis of *Cat's Eye*

Elaine Risley is a middle-aged, successful Canadian artist living in Vancouver, in the 1980s. She returns to her hometown, Toronto, to appear at a retrospective exhibition of her paintings. During her trip, she muses on her childhood and young-adult life, in particular her pre-pubescent years and her complicated relationship with her former best friend, Cordelia. The book is virtually a complete and chronological personal history of Elaine, detailing her romantic relationships, her unorthodox family and her entry into the art world. The association with Cordelia is, however, the main narrative subject, and even during the time when Cordelia is not present in Elaine's life, her influence is strongly felt.

Character summaries

Elaine Risley

Elaine is the main character and the narrator of *Cat's Eye*. She was born prior to World War II, and is the daughter of a homemaker and a forest entomologist (a scientist who studies insects). Her early childhood is very unusual, as she and her mother and brother travel around with her father during his research trips in northern Ontario, even during the War, when car travel was restricted due to petrol rationing. Because of this travel, Elaine and her brother are mainly home-schooled by their mother until the family is based in Toronto.

When they settle in Toronto, eight-year-old Elaine has trouble adjusting socially, feeling far more comfortable with the outdoor, unstructured environment of her early childhood. Elaine's difficulty in feeling as if she belongs is a problem that follows her throughout her life.

The defining experience in Elaine's life is the relationship she has with Cordelia, a neighbour and schoolmate. Cordelia bullies Elaine in a subtle, psychological way, eroding Elaine's self-esteem and causing her to become extremely anxious. Elaine turns to self-harm to manage her anxiety, peeling skin off her feet to the point of bleeding. Elaine's relationship with her parents, particularly with her mother, suffers during the period of Cordelia's bullying; Elaine is disappointed by her mother's inability to protect her.

Elaine is intelligent and does well in school. She attends the University of Toronto and takes classes in Art and Archaeology because she is interested in art but unsure how to pursue it practically. She does enrol in night classes at the Toronto College of Art (now known as the Ontario College of Art and Design), an important event that launches her career as a painter.

Elaine has an affair with her art teacher, Josef Hrbik, but eventually marries a fellow art student, Jon, after an unexpected pregnancy that results in the birth of their daughter, Sarah. Following a period of conflict and unhappiness in their marriage, Elaine slashes her wrist (after believing she hears the voice of Cordelia, urging her to do so). Shortly after this, Elaine leaves Jon, taking their daughter with her to Vancouver. Here she begins a period of recovery, not only from her marriage but also presumably from all the negative experiences she had in Toronto, including her torment at the hands of Cordelia and their mutual friends. It is during this time in Vancouver that Elaine's art career, which seemed mildly promising in Toronto, really picks up. Later, she marries again (a travel agent named Ben) and has a second child.

As an adult, Elaine has no close female friends.

Cordelia

Cordelia is the last girl to join the social group made up of Carol, Grace and Elaine, all of whom attend the same school. She is the youngest of three daughters, and moves with her family to Toronto one summer when Elaine and her family are away on one of Professor Risley's research trips.

Cordelia's body changes often through the narrative, but she is originally described as tall and thin with dark blonde hair and a crooked upper lip. While compelling, unlike her two sisters she is not traditionally beautiful. She is one year older than Elaine and, at first, is a year ahead in school. It is clear through details of her home and activities that Cordelia's family is more affluent than those of the other girls.

As a pre-pubescent girl, Cordelia is at first very friendly to Elaine. Soon though, she begins to bully Elaine in subtle ways, becoming more and more abusive and controlling until Elaine is suffering severe anxiety.

Cordelia is not presented as entirely negative – she is inventive and creative, and also ambitious in many ways. She has much more imagination than Elaine's other friends and is a natural leader among her peers.

Cordelia is not seen in a coherent, continual way throughout the narrative. Instead she appears after long absences, usually in a dramatically changed form, both physically and socially. This pattern may be the reason that the adult Elaine seems to constantly expect Cordelia to appear from nowhere.

Grace Smeath

Grace is, like Cordelia, a year older than Elaine and a year ahead in school. Grace is a very literal person, even as a child, and dislikes games involving imaginary elements – she prefers to play 'school' in the basement (with herself as teacher and Carol and Elaine as students) or to cut photos out of the Eaton's Catalogue.

Grace's family is considerably less affluent than the other girls', although this is not clear to them when they are young. The Smeath family is very religious and rigid, and these characteristics are dominant in Grace. Grace eventually leaves the group to go to a high school specialising in maths, causing Elaine to remark disparagingly, 'She's good at adding things up in neat little rows' (p.238). She and Elaine never see one another again.

Grace's role in the bullying of Elaine is less active than Cordelia's; she does not initiate the torment, but she aligns herself with Cordelia and participates in the bullying once it has begun. Grace is presented as seeming entirely unemotional, and as being indifferent to Elaine's pain, rather than interested in it as Cordelia appears to be. Despite these characteristics, Elaine, Carol and even Cordelia crave Grace's approval, especially early in their friendship. It is often said by Elaine that Grace held power because 'we want to play with her more than she wants to play with us' (p.61).

Grace is described as pale and freckled with frizzy brown hair that she wears in braids.

Carol Campbell

Carol Campbell is Elaine's first female friend. They are thrown together because they are in the same grade at school and live close to one another. It is through Carol that Elaine gains insight into what is considered normal in her new hometown. Carol introduces Elaine to Grace, and later the two of them introduce her to Cordelia.

Carol is a flighty, expressive, emotional child and in this she exhibits many stereotypical female characteristics that Elaine disdains. Her physicality conveniently matches these traits; she is described as blonde and stubby, with curled hair.

When Cordelia begins bullying Elaine, Carol is generally not an active participant, though she does nothing to protect or defend Elaine. She is in fact a target of the bullying herself at times, but unlike Elaine she is easily pushed to tears and exclamations of distress and therefore does not present a challenge to Cordelia.

Elaine's father (Mr Risley)

Elaine's father is an entomologist, which means he studies insects. Until Elaine is about eight, he works in the field, travelling around northern Ontario and studying bugs in their natural environment. Later he transitions to working as a professor at the University of Toronto.

Elaine has a more open relationship with her father than most girls in her generation; he treats her more or less as an equal, talking to her about scientific and environmental concerns. He is concerned with people's abilities, not their gender or race, and is quite enlightened in this sense. However, he assumes that other people think the same way he does and is surprised and disappointed on occasions when he realises that other people hold irrational prejudices. For example, when Dr Banerji, his Indian colleague, returns to India after suffering discrimination, Elaine observes: 'My father's view of human nature has always been bleak, but scientists were excluded from it, and now they aren't. He feels betrayed' (p.339).

Elaine's mother (Mrs Risley)

An unorthodox and modern woman, Elaine's mother is confident and grounded. She likes to wear casual or even men's clothes for comfort, and is at ease being outside and active, such as during the research excursions for her husband's job. However, she is also traditional in many ways. She does not work outside the home and she prepares the food and does the housework in the Risley household, albeit in her own slapdash way. Her relationship with her husband however, seems to be that of equals and advanced for the time.

Elaine's mother suffers a miscarriage when Elaine is a child, after they have moved to Toronto. This incident (though not fully understood by Elaine at the time) is Elaine's first instance of seeing her mother as anything but invincible.

Stephen Risley

Elaine's older brother is a brilliant scholar who is a close ally to Elaine in the years during and prior to World War II. As a child, he is bright and well-adjusted; however, he becomes increasingly unreadable to Elaine as he gets older and becomes more and more successful as a scholar, and later, as a scientist.

Stephen leaves Toronto to pursue his academic and scientific career and Elaine loses track of him. He marries and later divorces without explanation, informing Elaine via postcards.

Elaine and Stephen have only one interaction as adults in the book, when she attends a lecture he is giving about the birth of the universe. While they are friendly, it is clear that they have lost the tender connection of their shared childhood.

Stephen is killed during a terrorist attack on a commercial plane, on which he is a passenger. He is executed by the terrorists by being thrown from the plane. This incident has a traumatic effect on Elaine's parents, who never fully recover from the loss of their child.

A statement by Stephen opens the book, highlighting his importance to Elaine.

BACKGROUND & CONTEXT

Historical setting

Set in Canada during World War II and up to the mid-1980s, *Cat's Eye* covers several extremely influential historical events during its narrative. These include World War II; the death of King George VI; the second wave of the feminist movement; Canada's evolution from a country strongly controlled by British influence to an independent nation (including the adoption of the modern Canadian flag, the Maple Leaf) and several movements in the visual arts. All of these events are presented through the lens of the first-person narrator, artist Elaine Risley. As in several of Atwood's other novels, there are also brief references to the arrival of American draft dodgers in Toronto during the Vietnam War.

Cat's Eye examines gender roles without advocating any particular interpretation of how either gender is meant to behave. However, the issue of gender roles was of particular interest in the 1980s, when women began to make up a significant portion of the professional world and achieved high-ranking positions, arguably for the first time in significant numbers. Issues of interest included sexual harassment, hiring quotas (known in Canada as 'affirmative action') and the suggestion of a 'glass ceiling' for professional women (a term meaning that while there were no official policies preventing qualified women from being promoted, they were discriminated against regardless). Atwood, as a successful woman in what had once been a traditionally male field, has been considered to bring a unique viewpoint to gender-related issues. Some of the personal conflicts in the narrative allude to larger social conflicts regarding different opinions of what men and women's roles in society ought to be.

Places in *Cat's Eye*

Toronto

Toronto, the capital of the province of Ontario in Canada, is where Elaine spends much of her childhood, and where she has returned as an adult at the opening of *Cat's Eye*. She has a tormented relationship with the city, remembering it as the place where her childhood friend Cordelia and their mutual friends bullied and humiliated her. Elaine arrived in Toronto as a small child when her father, an entomologist, moved from field research to take up a university professorship. The adult Elaine categorises the many ways in which Toronto has changed when she returns for a retrospective exhibition of her artwork. Toronto is the biggest city in Canada, and the fifth largest in North America.

Northern Ontario

This is the area far north of Toronto in the province of Ontario, Canada. It is largely forested, with many small lakes. Elaine spent much of her time as a child travelling around northern Ontario with her father, mother and brother, Stephen. The north represented peace and safety to her, and she was comfortable with the family's rootless, nomadic existence, often feeling like an imposter later while trying to fit into the accepted mode of city living. When Elaine is older, her parents sell their house in Toronto and move to Sault Ste. Marie, a town in northern Ontario.

Vancouver

Vancouver, the capital of the province of British Columbia, Canada, is where Elaine moves when she leaves her first husband, Jon. She takes their daughter Sarah and travels there by train, as a plane flight would have been financially prohibitive at the time. Vancouver represents an unblemished future; the opportunity to put the past behind her and achieve the peace she is seeking.

Vancouver is very picturesque, with both ocean and mountain views and has very progressive environmental policies. It is the eighth largest city in Canada, the third largest by metropolitan area.

Author's historical context

Cat's Eye is Atwood's seventh novel (it was published three years after her famous dystopian novel, *The Handmaid's Tale*) and approximately her 27th book including her fiction, short story collections, poetry collections, children's books and non-fiction. At the time of its publication, Atwood was 49 years old and already an extremely well-known author, both in her home country of Canada, and internationally. Atwood began *Cat's Eye* very early in her career but put it aside until the mid-1980s.

Publishing context/history

Though, as an author, Atwood has been resistant to labels, many consider her to be an important feminist writer. *Cat's Eye* is relevant in this context, as it explores issues concerning women's political and personal identities as well as examining second-wave feminism.

Second-wave feminism was a social movement that began in the 1960s. Unlike earlier feminism, it focused on personal and cultural disparity as well as political and legal inequalities between the sexes. Carol Hanisch coined the phrase 'the personal is the political' to explain that inequity may remain in society despite the fact that women are legally eligible to vote, hold office, own and inherit property, and so on.

In *Cat's Eye,* Atwood's protagonist, Elaine, attends women's groups hosted by feminist activists. Through Elaine, Atwood examines the benefits and challenges associated with second wave feminism. Later in the narrative, when the timeline has progressed to the 1980s, there is also a brief examination of how changing gender roles have created both confusion and more freedom for young men and women. *Cat's Eye* questions and deconstructs the widely-held belief that women are inherently (by nature) nurturing, empathetic and influenced by emotion by exposing the cruelties perpetrated by Cordelia, Grace, Mrs. Smeath and even Elaine herself at times.

Though the assertion is unconfirmed, *Cat's Eye* is widely believed to be Atwood's most autobiographical novel to date. Her main character Elaine and she share several basic biographical details such as approximate age, hometown (the Leaside area of Toronto), parents' professions and artistic success (Elaine as a painter, Atwood as a writer). Like Elaine, Atwood spent much of her young life travelling around northern Ontario with her parents for her fathers' job as an entomologist.

GENRE, STRUCTURE & LANGUAGE

Genre

Cat's Eye can generally be described as postmodern literary fiction. Postmodernism is a critical school of thought that emerged in the decades following the end of World War II. While there is some debate on the exact nature of postmodernism and postmodern literature, it is generally interpreted as including books in which a quest for truth or insight is not seen as objective or absolute; rather, postmodernism calls into question categorical truths and a postmodernist interpreter would be more likely to see all issues and revelations as relative. Atwood plays with these concepts by having different characters remember and interpret the same events in very different ways (particularly the characters of Elaine and Cordelia, but also Elaine and her brother Stephen and Elaine and her mother). Atwood, however, has at times resisted the label 'postmodern' being applied to her work.

Literary fiction is another somewhat loaded term whereby not everyone agrees on its definition. Generally, literary fiction is considered fiction in which the quality of prose and the depth of narrative complexity signify a work of fine art, beyond that of a book written simply for entertainment.

More specifically, *Cat's Eye* is a *Bildungsroman*, a genre that follows a character from childhood to adulthood and highlights the change that has taken place. In the case of Elaine Risley, the central character, the main change is emotional; there is hope that Elaine has found a place in which she feels she belongs, after a long period of feeling as though she did not fit neatly into any category or community she came across. Atwood tweaks this structure slightly by leaving ambiguous whether or not Elaine is in fact at peace, prompting the reader to examine how and to what extent people are able to change and to overcome the effects of childhood events.

The novel is the story of Elaine's life and is told in her voice. This is important, as it implies that the reader is only aware of Elaine's version of events. The storyline is therefore limited to what Elaine knows of any given situation, and much information is purposefully omitted because Elaine could not possibly be aware of it (for instance, Cordelia's motivations are never specifically revealed, though much can be guessed at from the information provided).

Cat's Eye can also be considered a *Künstlerroman*, since it depicts the development and maturation of an artist. Elaine's early artistic tendencies can be observed throughout the book, and her artwork clearly reflects pivotal experiences in her life – several of the sections are given the same names of her paintings. Since Atwood pays particular attention to the actual paintings, which are described in detail, in order to communicate information about the character, and since an exhibition of Elaine's paintings is the central event of the 'present day' sections of the book, *Cat's Eye* fits very neatly into the *Künstlerroman* definition. In addition, Elaine's artistic training is described in detail, further contributing to this classification.

Structure

There are fifteen sections in *Cat's Eye* and each section opens with a chapter in the novel's current day, some time in the 1980s. This is followed by chapters which flash back to describe the earlier life of the narrator, Elaine Risley, in chronological order, which include Elaine's experience of several significant historical events.

The most notable exception to this structure is the first section, titled 'Iron Lung'. This section is made up of two short chapters, the first of which is only a single page long. While it is also part of the narrative, its main function is to introduce the reader to the themes and concerns of the novel, namely time and memory. The second short chapter of the first section opens with a short scene Elaine is remembering from her childhood involving her friend Cordelia. The same chapter goes on to talk about Elaine's current feelings for Cordelia, which are complicated. This is the only portion of the book that mixes the two timelines in a single chapter, and it echoes the theme of the opening chapter, which is the fluidity of time and the difficulty of keeping the past in the past.

Language

Cat's Eye is written entirely in the present tense, a somewhat unusual choice as the majority of novels are written in the past tense. It is also one of the few of Atwood's novels written from the first person perspective; she usually opts for the third person perspective. The present tense being applied to both the past and also to Elaine's present (during her visit to Toronto) conveys the feeling that the past is as immediate to her as the present, and echoes the theme of the book's opening, where Elaine says 'Time is not a line but a dimension, like the dimensions of space. If you can bend space you can bend time also' (p.3).

Time and the memory of times gone by are extremely important to the novel; by presenting all events in the present tense, Atwood communicates that, to Elaine, the time in which something has happened is virtually irrelevant. Instead it is the effect of the event that matters.

The first person perspective also allows readers to call into question Elaine's version of events. At first, everything Elaine says can be assumed to be true; however, as other characters offer different versions of events, readers may become uncertain of the accuracy of Elaine's memories.

The linguistic style of the writing is typical of Atwood's novels that are set in contemporary periods. It is a direct and descriptive voice, and often displays an interest in language itself, for instance when Elaine categorises boys and girls at her high school according to the slang of the day (p.245), or makes up curse words with her brother as a form of bonding (p.258). When Elaine is comparing the time of her adult life to her life as a child and noting the many changes that have taken place, she analyses language as an example of change: 'I'm lying on the floor, on a futon, covered by a duvet. *Futon, duvet*: this is how far we've come' (p.13). By drawing together language and time, Atwood uses language to support her main themes of time and memory.

SECTION-BY-SECTION ANALYSIS

Section I: Iron Lung

The first section of *Cat's Eye* opens with a page-long chapter in which Elaine discusses the nature of time and reveals her obsession with her past and her inability to make sense of the things that have happened in her life. Unlike other chapters, it is not clear how old Elaine is when she is speaking in this chapter.

The second chapter in 'Iron Lung' describes Elaine and her friend Cordelia taking a streetcar ride from their home in residential Toronto to the downtown core. They are thirteen years old in this scene and think they are best friends.

Key point

Cordelia and Elaine observe and give their opinions of different women on the streetcar, highlighting Elaine's lifelong fascination and difficulties with women and girls.

The chapter goes on in the voice of the adult Elaine, who has returned to Toronto to attend an exhibition of her paintings. Elaine reveals that she is no longer in contact with Cordelia and is unaware of what has happened to her. She also reveals her intensely complex feelings about Cordelia, picturing Cordelia in a variety of unpleasant situations, including Cordelia as a mentally-ill, homeless woman, or alternatively in an iron lung, from which the section name is taken. An iron lung is a machine that enables a person suffering from polio, for example, to breathe. A patient in an iron lung is completely immobilised and helpless, a situation with which Elaine identifies.

Q Why does Atwood open by talking about time? How does time feature in Elaine's life?

Q Elaine and Cordelia are 13-years-old in their first appearance in the book. What is unique about that point in their relationship?

Section II: Silver Paper

The adult Elaine is staying in the empty studio apartment of her ex-husband, Jon, in Toronto. She reflects on the way Toronto has changed since she moved to British Columbia. While in Jon's studio, Elaine reminisces about the constructions Jon made when they were both young artists. Unlike Elaine, Jon has not been successful in his art career and has shifted to creating special effects props for movies, specialising in artificial body parts and violence; pieces of his work litter the studio.

Elaine walks towards the gallery that is presenting the retrospective of her work and thinks about growing older. On the street, she sees a poster advertising the exhibition, with a moustache drawn on to her face. Rather than being upset by this, she sees the graffiti as a sign that she has become more prominent than she ever expected.

In Chapter 4, the time frame shifts to Elaine's childhood. She describes her life during World War II, travelling around northern Ontario with her family on her father's research trips. She sits alone in the back seat, looking at her parents and brother from behind. This is, chronologically, the youngest Elaine the reader sees. It is significant however, that even during this happy time the very first presentation of Elaine shows her as literally isolated; alone in the back seat. She is observing her family rather than interacting with them. Later, when she is bullied, Elaine is forced to be the studied rather than the studier, and she is extremely uncomfortable with such scrutiny.

Key point

Elaine is always more comfortable in the role of an observer than a participant, which may be one reason she is drawn to painting and art later in life as a way of expressing herself. Observation is how Elaine feels in control.

Chapter 4 describes the family's typical routine, sleeping in tents, eating at a campfire, occasionally staying in motels or cabins. Elaine relates her close relationship with her brother. As one another's only playmates, they spend much of their time together. Her brother, Stephen, engages in behaviour typical of young boys, playing with planes, making toy weapons, looking at bugs in the forest and playing 'war' with Elaine.

During these games of war, Stephen always wins and Elaine must pretend to be dead. This biddable nature of Elaine's foreshadows the ease with which Cordelia is later able to control her.

In Chapter 5, World War II ends and Elaine has her eighth birthday, receiving a camera as a gift. Elaine and Stephen draw pictures – he of wars and she of little girls in long dresses with puffed sleeves. The pictures reflect Elaine's desire for friends of her own age and gender. In the winter, Elaine and her family move to their new house in Toronto, a yellow brick bungalow in a newly developed neighbourhood. It becomes clear that the contractor for the house has left in the middle of the project, without approval; the house is largely unfinished. Elaine's mother maintains a positive attitude, whereas her father is more irritated by the situation. Upon seeing the state of the new house, Elaine goes into the bathroom to avoid letting her parents see how upset she is. She says 'I feel trapped. I want to be back in the motel, back on the road, in my old rootless life of impermanence and safety' (p.36). As time passes, Elaine's first observation of her new life is the change in the way her parents dress, which seems to be a symbol of their acceptance of more traditional gender roles while living in the city.

On Saturdays Elaine and Stephen go to their father's office in the Zoology Building at the University of Toronto (which they refer to as 'the building'). It is a positive space for Elaine, where she and Stephen can resume their games and exploring. From the building, Elaine watches the Santa Claus parade, an annual event. She is disappointed by Santa Claus, who she observes is 'smaller than expected' (p.42). In this and many other small ways, Toronto continues to be a source of disappointment to her.

Section II – 'Silver Paper' – takes its name from the silver paper from cigarette packages which Elaine collects, intending to use it for a craft activity of some sort. She is unsure what she will use it for but saves the paper anyway. This is another early suggestion of her artistic leanings.

Q Why is 'the building' a place where Elaine is comfortable?

Q The role of observer appeals to Elaine. Why is that? What roles do the other family members play?

Section III: Empire Bloomers

As the first chapter in section III, Chapter 8 returns to the adult Elaine visiting Toronto. She struggles with an unnamed problem, which may be depression or a similar affliction, noting 'there are days when I can hardly make it out of bed' (p.47). She recalls conversations with Cordelia: '*What do you have to say for yourself?* Cordelia used to ask. *Nothing,* I would say.' She then reflects: 'It was a word I came to connect with myself' (p.47).

Key point

It is clear that both Cordelia and the experiences they had when they were friends continue to affect Elaine, even as an adult, in an extremely visceral way.

Elaine calls her husband, Ben, when she feels overwhelmed. She then shops for a dress, being unsatisfied with the one she has brought from home. While she is in the fitting room, someone attempts to steal the wallet from her purse through the gap under the door. She stomps on the hand and the thief drops the wallet. Elaine hears girls laughing and tries to catch them, but they are gone. Elaine's reaction is '*Damn you, Cordelia!* ... But Cordelia is long gone' (p.51), suggesting that although Elaine has been unable to find Cordelia, she worries that she might appear anywhere at anytime. It is also notable that she still thinks of Cordelia as a young girl, showing that time is relative for Elaine.

Back in her childhood, Elaine is sent to school. The school has separate doors for boys and for girls. These doors hold great mystery for Elaine. Elaine is befriended by a girl named Carol Campbell. They walk to and from school together and Carol invites Elaine over to her house. Carol has stereotypical feminine interests such as clothing, hairstyles and romance. Carol is expressive and cheerful and when Elaine invites her over, she observes the Risleys' unfinished house with 'incredulous glee' (p.57) and gossips at school about it and the unusual habits of Elaine's parents. Elaine says of this act 'She doesn't repeat these items with scorn, but as exotic specialties' (p.57). In this sense, Carol is actually one of the most accepting characters in the book; she observes Elaine's differences but finds them harmless.

Elaine takes Carol to 'the building', where Carol is disgusted by most of the experiments and scientific apparatus. Elaine begins to realise that this squeamish attitude is what is expected of girls, and feels freakish. She longs for a friend more like herself.

Carol introduces Elaine to Grace Smeath, another neighbourhood girl who attends the same school but who is one year older. Grace comes from a deeply religious family and is very rigid. Together the three girls play games of Grace's choosing. Summarising the relationship between the three girls, Elaine observes 'Because we want to play with [Grace] more than she wants to play with us, she gets her way in everything' (p.61). Later, Elaine meets Grace's mother, a plain and imposing woman who has, according to Grace, a bad heart. Elaine describes her in detail (p.67) as a raw and unattractive woman. It is clear she is a very significant person to Elaine, but Elaine herself is unsure why, saying, 'Why do I hate her so much? Why do I care, in any way, what went on in her head?' (p.68).

As spring approaches, Carol and Grace teach Elaine other typical pastimes for girls their age, such as skipping rope and ball games. Marbles becomes a popular pursuit at school for both girls and boys. Stephen becomes extremely good at winning marbles from other children and eventually has a collection so large that he buries his best ones as 'treasure'. Elaine, for the first time, has trouble understanding him. She, too, enjoys marbles and is particularly fond of her blue cat's eye marble, a type of marble that has a coloured swirl in the middle.

Key point

Elaine enjoys having an activity (marbles) that is engaged in by both boys and girls, easing her discomfort about fitting into the world of little girls.

Elaine and her family return to the north for the summer so her father can do further research. She readjusts to her previous life without trouble, and indeed her life during the school year in Toronto seems to be only a vague memory. When she returns to Toronto at the end of the summer, Elaine says that the neighbours 'stare as if we're new people, as if I've never lived here' (p.81). Grace and Carol are waiting for her and there is a new girl with them: Cordelia. Soon the girls are all spending time together. Elaine describes Cordelia's home life, which is elegant and affluent. She has two older sisters named Perdita and Miranda, who are affectionately called Perrie and Mirrie. Unlike her sisters, Cordelia is always called by her full name, highlighting how she is treated differently than her sisters and less favoured. Cordelia prefers much more imaginative games than those that Grace has dictated the group play up to this point.

There is a bridge in a ravine which the girls walk over everyday going to and from school. Cordelia scares the other girls by telling them that the river below is made of dead people because it flows out of the cemetery.

Elaine is in her second year at school in Toronto, with Carol in her class and Cordelia and Grace in the year ahead. Elaine's new teacher, Miss Lumley, is harsh and Elaine is frightened of her.

Q Cordelia is different from the other girls. In what ways is she similar to Elaine? In what ways are they different?

Q Atwood describes the family life of each of the four girls as being very different. What effect does each girl's family life appear to have on her?

Q Elaine shows in this section that her memory is not always reliable. What impact does this have on your reading?

Section IV: Deadly Nightshade

At Sub-Versions, the gallery hosting her show, the adult Elaine examines some of her paintings and the reader learns that Mrs Smeath is the subject of at least one of these. She meets Charna, the gallery director, and is introduced to, and interviewed by, a young journalist, Andrea. Elaine was not given warning about this interview and, though she agrees to it, is difficult and uncooperative during the process, dismissing Andrea as too young to understand a woman of her own generation. However, Elaine is also genuinely nervous and intimidated, and her lack of cooperation seems to be a coping mechanism.

Key point

Elaine also resists the journalist's interpretation of her work as categorically feminist, saying 'I hate party lines, I hate ghettoes' (p.105). This can be interpreted as the author speaking, resisting a strictly feminist reading of Cat's Eye.

Back in Elaine's childhood, Cordelia changes the dynamic of the girls' social group, ridiculing their games and introducing new ones. Mrs Smeath invites Elaine to attend church with the Smeath family and Elaine goes, despite her atheist parents' reservations. While feeling slightly disoriented at first, Elaine generally enjoys the church experience, saying: 'I feel included, taken in. God loves me, whoever he is' (p.116). After church the Smeath family, including Grace's Aunt Mildred, a retired missionary, and Elaine go to the train tracks to watch the trains. They then eat Sunday dinner, where Mr Smeath makes a slightly rude joke, showing himself to be of a very different demeanour from the women in his family. At school, Elaine observes more of the differences between the behaviour of, and the established roles for, boys and girls. She also finds out, to her surprise, that Stephen has a crush on a girl. She is disappointed in him as she feels the infatuation is beneath his dignity.

Key point

Elaine has internalised the idea that there is something inferior about girls, which is why she is disappointed that Stephen has a crush. Yet she sees herself in a different light, different from girls like Carol, whom she judges.

Cordelia digs a hole in her backyard while the other girls wrap Elaine in a sheet, pretending she is Mary, Queen of Scots. They then 'bury' her and leave her down in the hole for a very long time. Elaine is terrified but notes that she can't remember whether or not she was crying when they eventually let her out. Shortly after this, she turns nine years of age. The voice of the adult Elaine intrudes into this chapter, as she tries to remember the birthday party from that year. Instead, all she can remember is an image of deadly nightshade, the poisonous plant which represents the poison that Cordelia's presence was in her life.

Key point

Elaine's incomplete memories in this chapter again show that her version of events is possibly unreliable.

Q Elaine is judgmental of other girls. What does she dislike about them and why? Is she being fair in her judgment?

Q Mrs Smeath is a very important character. What does she represent for Elaine? Why does Elaine choose to paint her?

Section V: Wringer

Adult Elaine leaves the gallery and continues her stream of observations about modern Toronto. She goes to Simpson's department store, a place she remembers from childhood, to get something to eat. In Simpson's, which has changed significantly from the way she remembers it, Elaine thinks of the time when Cordelia 'had such power over' her (p.134). She recalls peeling the skin off her feet until they bled, as well as chewing on her hair and biting off the skin around her fingernails. Elaine also remembers how worried she was when she had daughters (rather than sons), and how surprised she was that her daughters seemed much more resilient than she had been as a child, saying: 'They seemed to have been born with some kind of protective coating, some immunity I lacked' (p.135).

In the past, Cordelia and the other girls bully Elaine, isolating her and maintaining she has done something wrong but not telling her what it is. They hide this behaviour from their parents, while constantly berating Elaine when they are alone, insisting she is abnormal and freakish. Elaine tries to avoid the girls by staying home more often. Sometimes Cordelia picks Carol as her victim instead, but usually it is Elaine. Elaine continues to attend Sunday School with Grace, who reports on her behaviour to Cordelia. Miss Lumley, Elaine's teacher, notes that Elaine's handwriting is deteriorating. Christmas comes, and Elaine's father brings home a graduate student, Mr Banerji, an academic from India. Elaine is hired by Mrs Finestein, her next-door neighbour, to take Mrs. Finestein's baby son, Brian, out for walks in his stroller. Elaine soon quits, however, worried that the other girls would convince her to allow Brian to be hurt. She also learns that the Finesteins are Jewish. Mrs. Finestein, who is kind to Elaine, is another one of the figures (in addition to Mr. Banjeri and later Miss Stuart) who emerge during Elaine's darkest time, and with whom Elaine identifies.

The bullying continues until one day at school, while spending time with the other girls, Elaine vomits and is allowed to go home. After this, she is sick more often, feeling it is a good way to escape from Cordelia and the others. Spring comes and the girls skip rope and play marbles again. Elaine finds her cat's eye marble and carries it with her as a protective talisman. The summer comes and Elaine is relieved to go north with her parents and Stephen again.

Q Why is the adult Elaine so concerned with cataloguing the ways that Toronto has changed?

Q How does the bullying Elaine experiences differ from the way boys bully one another?

Section VI: Cat's Eye

Intimidated by the renovated Simpson's store, Elaine leaves without eating. On the street, she is accosted by a homeless woman, to whom she gives ten dollars.

When the young Elaine returns to the city, Cordelia begins tormenting her again, more relentlessly than before. Elaine considers suicide, claiming that she doesn't really want to hurt herself but that she hears Cordelia's voice in her head urging her to do so. She says: 'I would be doing these things to please her' (p.185). Elaine also mentions that she considers telling Stephen what is happening but feels he won't understand. Later, Elaine's mother makes gives her advice that makes it clear she knows something is going on but confesses that she doesn't know how to stop it or exactly what it is. When the girls play doctor, Elaine, compelled by them to touch Carol's developing breasts, is nauseated by the evidence of Carol's emerging sexuality. Elaine's mother suffers a miscarriage and is rushed to the hospital in the middle of the night. Her mother's ill health and her inability to protect Elaine change Elaine's perception of her mother; she realises her mother is not invincible.

Elaine has a new kind-hearted teacher, Miss Stuart, whom, even though she is unable to protect her, Elaine adores. Miss Stuart has the students paint and draw in class, awakening Elaine's love of art. The class paints murals of different countries and of people who live there.

Key point

Elaine sees art as a way out of her misery, saying: 'If these people exist I can go there sometime. I don't have to stay here' (p.192).

Elaine and her brother attend an exhibition at the zoology building, where several experiments are open to the public. While in a hot room, Elaine faints and her father takes her home. Cordelia continues tormenting Elaine, constantly berating her for every perceived error. In the schoolyard, Elaine faints again and finds that fainting can be useful to her; it is a way of escaping from Cordelia.

Q How does Elaine's relationship with her mother change in this section?

Q What does art represent for Elaine?

Section VII: Our Lady of Perpetual Help

Adult Elaine goes back to Jon's studio and looks in the Toronto phone book for people she used to know, including Cordelia, but is unable to find any of them listed. She remembers the turbulent beginning of her relationship with Jon, with whom she is scheduled to have lunch while in Toronto.

As a child, Elaine overhears Grace's mother and Aunt Mildred talking about her, in a conversation where they acknowledge they are aware of the other girls' mistreatment of Elaine and that they approve of it, observing: 'It's God's punishment' and 'It serves her right' (p.213). After this, Elaine no longer feels welcome at church, and begins praying to the Virgin Mary instead, an act considered blasphemous by the Protestant church.

While walking home from school in the snow, Cordelia throws Elaine's hat down into the river from the bridge over which they walk everyday. She tells Elaine to get it, adding: 'Then you'll be forgiven' (p.221). Elaine does go down, but she falls into the frozen river and the other girls leave her there. Elaine struggles but begins to lose consciousness once she pulls herself out. She hallucinates an image of the Virgin Mary floating above the bridge before she manages to get up from the riverbank. As she stumbles towards her house her mother finds her and takes her home in a panic. When Elaine returns to school, after two days at home recovering, Cordelia tries to resume bullying her, but she is unwilling to continue to be a victim. The girls try to shame and taunt Elaine into rejoining them, but she is resolute. She stops attending church with Grace, ignores the other girls and eventually makes a new friend named Jill.

Q Why do Mrs Smeath and her sister feel so justified in their approval of the girls' bullying of Elaine? What does this say about them?

Q Why does Elaine see the Virgin Mary when she is freezing?

Section VIII: Half a Face

The adult Elaine notes her compulsion to go into churches, and how it took her a long time to realise it was because she was searching for the version of the Virgin Mary she saw while she was freezing. She eventually finds a statue of her in a church in Mexico; she is known as the Virgin of lost things.

Back in Elaine's childhood, the King of England dies and Princess Elizabeth takes the throne as Queen. Elaine goes to a new school closer to her home; the other girls go too but she still refuses to socialise with them. The narrative time speeds up considerably in this section. Cordelia and Grace skip a grade, then graduate and go to high school. Elaine gets a boyfriend, about whom she seems absent-minded. She too skips a grade. She finds that she barely remembers Cordelia and the others, and is even unable to remember the significance of the cat's eye marble when she comes across it. Indeed, Elaine has become independent and unshakable, much more stable than her pubescent peers, from whom she feels very separate.

Key point

Again, Elaine feels different from her peers and emotionally detached, never seeming to be quite comfortable with what is expected from her according to her age or gender.

Before Elaine's first day of high school, Cordelia's mother calls and asks if Elaine will walk to school with Cordelia. Elaine agrees to this as if it holds no significance for her. Cordelia has been expelled from her private high school and she and Elaine are now in the same grade. Elaine and Cordelia are friends as if nothing has ever happened between them. While Cordelia struggles both academically and socially in grade nine, Elaine has no trouble adjusting to high school, saying: 'I am calm; I regard the antics of my fellow students ... with a combination of scientific curiosity and almost matronly indulgence' (p.245). Cordelia shoplifts and behaves like a typical teen while Elaine maintains her detached manner.

Stephen goes to a private boys' school for gifted students and has become distant from Elaine. Obviously brilliant, he is already preoccupied with scientific pursuits. Elaine goes away with her parents again for the summer, receiving letters from both Stephen and Cordelia.

Q Time moves much faster in this section than previous ones. Why does Atwood devote more time to Elaine's childhood than her teenage years?

Q Why do Elaine and Cordelia behave so differently as teenagers?

Section IX: Leprosy

Charna calls Elaine from the gallery to let her know that the interview with Andrea has been published. Elaine reads it and is unsatisfied, but she hopes that Cordelia will see it and come to the exhibition, despite knowing this is not realistically likely.

Elaine and Cordelia, now in grade ten, walk in Mount Pleasant Cemetery, where Elaine scares Cordelia with a story about being a vampire. This is the point where Elaine feels she has become stronger than Cordelia and is now the dominant one in the friendship. Around the same time, Elaine develops a reputation for being sharp-tongued. The girls often banter, but there is an undertone of cruelty. Because Elaine is quicker and more intelligent, Cordelia usually ends up at a disadvantage in these situations. Both Cordelia and Elaine go out with boys, but Elaine is as detached in her romantic relationships as she is in all other social relationships.

A girl is found murdered in Elaine's neighbourhood. Later in the same year, Cordelia assists with a theatrical production, where an error with the props leaves her humiliated. Elaine mocks her about this rather than sympathising; she is shocked at her own behaviour, wondering why she would be cruel to her best friend, not consciously remembering Cordelia's mistreatment of her when they were younger. Cordelia tells Elaine that when she was younger she tried to make herself sick, much like Elaine did. She also tells Elaine she was unhappy as a young child and that Elaine was her only friend. It becomes apparent that not only are Elaine's own memories unreliable and inconsistent, but also that she and Cordelia have very different memories of their young lives together.

Key point

Elaine is often shown to have different memories from those of her friends and family, bringing into question whose version of events is actually true.

Elaine begins to avoid Cordelia, who continues to fail academically and soon moves away with her family. Elaine carries on as if nothing has happened, writes the grade thirteen exams and decides to be a painter. Cordelia calls, seeking a closer relationship with Elaine, who goes to see her in her new home. Elaine resists her overtures. All of this happens without either of them openly discussing it, but the implication is clear. Elaine leaves Cordelia and feels she is abandoning her.

Q Why is Elaine suddenly unwilling to be friends with Cordelia after she moves?

Q Why does the author include the story of the murdered girl? In what sense is the murdered girl a parallel for Elaine?

Section X: Life Drawing

Elaine has lunch with Jon, her ex-husband. They banter, talk about their daughter (Sarah) and Jon shares that his current wife has left him.

Now a high school graduate, Elaine takes an art class in life drawing at the Toronto College of Art with an instructor named Josef Hrbik. She can already draw well, but needs to learn to imbue her art with life and meaning. She is drawn to Josef who, as a recent immigrant, is another outsider. He shares some characteristics with Mr (now Dr) Banerji and Mrs Finestein.

Elaine also enrols at the University of Toronto to study Art and Archaeology and feels caught between the respectable world of her university course and the bohemian atmosphere of her life drawing classes.

Key point

Again, Elaine has trouble deciding where she fits in and where she belongs.

Elaine goes to a bar with some of her art class schoolmates, including Jon. She is comfortable having male friends, and resents it when Susie, another girl from class, joins them at the bar on another occasion. Elaine soon discovers that Susie is having an affair with Mr Hrbik.

Elaine reads existential literature while living at home. Dr Banerji goes back to India after experiencing discrimination at the University of Toronto. Stephen goes to California to study astrophysics and is detained by the military when he accidentally wanders into a restricted area. Elaine begins dating Josef and hears gossip that he is misrepresenting his intentions to Susie, whom he is still seeing. Elaine loses her virginity to Josef and spends the summer in Toronto, working at the Swiss Chalet, a down-market restaurant in the city. After several months of this, seeing Josef twice a week and living away from home, Elaine finds she is unhappy. At this vulnerable point, Cordelia again appears unexpectedly, asking Elaine to lunch. Cordelia has left home and is working at the Stratford Shakespeare Festival, a prestigious theatrical event. She is thinner, with a striking appearance and Elaine feels at a disadvantage. Cordelia gives her a ticket and Elaine goes to see her in a production of *The Tempest*. Meanwhile, Josef and Elaine continue to see each other and Elaine begins to find his melodrama tiring. Jon comes by Elaine's workplace and they go out for drinks. As he walks her home, she is overcome by sadness and begins to cry. Jon comforts her and takes her back to his apartment where they sleep together.

Q Elaine and Susie both have relationships with Josef. In what ways do they behave differently and why? In what ways are they similar?

Q How does Elaine's early art training influence her career as a painter?

Section XI: Falling Women

The adult Elaine walks north on University Avenue in Toronto, reminiscing about Josef. She is asked for money by a refugee woman and gives her ten dollars after momentarily mistaking her for Cordelia.

As a young woman, Elaine returns to university in fall (autumn) and continues to see Jon as well as Josef, who is still seeing Susie. Susie calls her one day asking her to come over. When Elaine arrives, she finds Susie unconscious and bloody; she is injured from an inexpertly performed abortion, having become pregnant to Josef. Elaine confronts Josef, angry on Susie's behalf. He is distraught when she stops seeing him. Elaine and Jon continue to date, although he has bohemian attitudes about monogamy, not wanting to be tied down. She accommodates this, not wanting to be seen as clingy. She continues painting, using egg tempera. Jon also creates art projects, though his work is avant-garde, unlike Elaine's more traditional methods.

Elaine graduates and gets a job painting advertisements. She moves into her own apartment, where Jon often stays. Elaine's parents move north, and Stephen sends postcards from his various homes, including news that he has married and, in a later correspondence, that he is divorced. Stephen comes to Toronto to deliver a lecture, which Elaine attends, though she understands little of the content. She reminisces with her brother afterwards, finding they have very different memories of their childhood.

Key point

Realising Stephen has different memories of their childhood causes Elaine to worry about the integrity of her own memories.

Elaine discovers she is pregnant by Jon. In shock, she begins to paint objects and people from her childhood, unsure of why she is doing so. Several years ahead in time, Elaine and Jon are married and their daughter Sarah is a toddler. Jon and Elaine begin to fight. Elaine attends a women's group, where she feels out of place. She and some of the women from her drawing group stage an art show. An all-female show is highly unusual at the time and attracts attention.

Elaine visits Cordelia in a mental hospital, where she is living. She is sedated and has trouble focusing when she and Elaine go out for lunch. She asks Elaine to get her out of the hospital, to give her money so she can leave, but Elaine refuses, worrying about the consequences of such a decision. Afterwards, Elaine has troublesome dreams of Cordelia. She never sees her again.

Q What does the section title refer to? Who are the falling women and how are they similar and different?

Q Why do Elaine and Stephen have such different memories from childhood?

Section XII: One Wing

Elaine eats in a diner with a 1940s theme and compares it in her mind to the real decade, again showcasing her obsession with time and change. She walks by Josef's old house and notes a film of his she saw at some point, which she interprets as being based on his relationships with her and Susie. Elaine later meets Jon at the rooftop bar of the Park Plaza Hotel, after which they go back to his studio and sleep together. Although they feel tenderly towards one another, they are clearly no longer in love.

Returning to the narrative of the past, Elaine and Jon continue to fight, more explosively than ever. After Jon storms out following a particularly vicious argument, Elaine cuts her wrist. Jon takes her to the hospital. Soon after, Jon comes home just as she and Sarah are leaving for Vancouver and although he is upset, he doesn't stop them. In Vancouver, Elaine is both relieved and depressed. Eventually she pulls herself together and continues her painting career. She meets Ben and they get married.

Q What motivates Elaine to constantly compare the present to the past?

Section XIII: Picoseconds

Elaine visits her old neighbourhood and wonders what life is like for the children who live there now.

In the past, Elaine describes Stephen's death, which took place during a terrorist attack on a commercial flight. She also describes her parents' inability to process Stephen's death. Later, Elaine's father dies and her mother becomes ill. Elaine goes to her parents' house to help her mother go through the house. She and her mother discuss Stephen, whom her mother remembers in an idealised way, and then the two of them obliquely discuss the bullying Elaine endured. Elaine's mother blames Grace, assuming Cordelia was not the instigator. While going through the house, Elaine finds her old cat's eye marble, and when she looks at it, all the memories she has repressed come flooding back. Later, Elaine goes to visit her old school and discovers it has been torn down.

Q What is the significance of Elaine's old school being torn down?

Q Elaine's parents start out as very certain and confident people, but later in life become unsure and have trouble understanding changes in the world. What is Atwood saying about the difficulties of aging? How is Elaine similar to her parents?

Section XIV: Unified Field Theory

The past and present narratives connect in this section. Elaine arrives early at the gallery and critically examines her paintings before the show begins. She reflects on what they represent and her motivation in creating them. She waits in the back room until the guests arrive and then peers through the crowd hoping Cordelia will show up, but she doesn't. The show is a success and Elaine returns to Jon's empty studio in a taxi. Slightly drunk, she makes herself coffee. She confronts her memories of Cordelia and cries.

Q What is the significance of the subjects Elaine has chosen for her paintings?

Section XV: Bridge

Elaine misses her return flight and goes back to the bridge where she almost froze to death as a child. The wooden bridge has been replaced with a concrete version. She thinks she sees Cordelia and imagines releasing her, saying: 'You can go home now' (p.496). Elaine then catches another flight home. She observes two older women on the plane and wishes she and Cordelia could have had the chance to grow old together.

Key point

Cordelia is the one person in Elaine's life to whom she was able to truly relate, a person similar to herself. In many ways the tragedy of the story is not just the negative experiences Elaine had, but the friendship that she and Cordelia could have had if only things had been slightly different. Instead, Elaine feels like an outsider for most of her life, without any close friends.

Q What is the significance of the title 'Bridge'?

Q Is the ending of the book hopeful or not?

CHARACTERS & RELATIONSHIPS

Elaine and Cordelia

Key quotes

'She creates a circle of two, takes me in' (p.83).

'This is what I miss, Cordelia: not something that's gone but something that will never happen' (p.498).

'I'm not afraid of seeing Cordelia. I'm afraid of being Cordelia' (p.267).

Relationship

The central relationship in *Cat's Eye* is that between the narrator, Elaine, and her childhood friend, Cordelia. Cordelia's constantly changing nature and behaviour exacerbates Elaine's difficulties with belonging. Cordelia's power games and manipulations when the girls are young cause Elaine to become extremely anxious and, at times, depressed. However, because Cordelia is extremely charming and charismatic, Elaine continues to crave her approval. Cordelia is sometimes kind to Elaine as well, causing Elaine to be confused and conflicted about the nature of their friendship. When Cordelia leaves Elaine in an icy river, Elaine hallucinates an image of the Virgin Mary. After this, Elaine finds she has the strength to rebuff Cordelia's bullying, and stops being friends with her.

When the two girls are brought together again in high school and become close friends, Elaine does not clearly remember her previous relationship with Cordelia. The power dynamic is different and Elaine slowly gains the upper hand. She often teases Cordelia, even about things she knows will bother her. Later, Elaine withholds affection, although she is aware that Cordelia will feel abandoned. Throughout the novel, the two are unable to interact in a positive way. Cordelia appears occasionally, and whenever she does Elaine either feels superior to her and guilty, or inferior to her and anxious. Cordelia is the only friend Elaine ever has who is particularly similar to her; like Elaine, she is creative and imaginative, but she lacks Elaine's self-control and sense of duty. Elaine both loves Cordelia for being brave enough to resist the domestic, typically female persona of the time (and therefore more like Elaine herself), and hates Cordelia for having been so cruel to her.

Cordelia is also the first proof Elaine has that imagination is a tool that can be wielded for good or evil. It can be used to entertain, to frighten or to control.

Key points

- Though Cordelia is at times a source of pain for Elaine, it is clear that Elaine admires Cordelia and her unique talents.
- Because Cordelia is inconsistent, Elaine is unsure how they ought to relate to one another; she constantly thinks Cordelia might show up unexpectedly.

Elaine and Grace Smeath

Key quote

'She never raises her voice, gets angry, or cries; she is quietly reproachful' (p.61).

Relationship

Grace introduces Elaine to religion and she is initially comfortable going to church with her despite the fact that Elaine's parents are atheists and she has never had any religious instruction. However, as Grace joins Cordelia in tormenting her, Elaine comes to see God as either a negative force, or simply another authority figure incapable of protecting her from her bullying friends. However, the Virgin Mary, to whom Elaine begins to pray during the worst of her troubles with the other girls, becomes an important figure in her life. In this sense, by introducing Elaine to religion, Grace has a very formative effect on her. Though Elaine is not religious in the conventional sense, she takes comfort and solace in the image of the Virgin Mary, who often features in her art work.

Grace's mother features more significantly in the adult Elaine's recollections than Grace herself; Grace's role as merely an 'assistant' in the young girls' mistreatment of Elaine leaves her eclipsed by Cordelia.

Key points

- Grace is a very static character. She is initially presented as rigid and literal and never wavers from that description.
- Because there is little mystery to her, she doesn't haunt Elaine the way Cordelia does.

Elaine and Carol Campbell

Key quotes

'She's a stubby girl with a frequent laugh' (p.55).

'There's a recklessness in [Carol], she can be pushed just so far, she has a weak sense of honour, she's reliable only as an informer' (p.143).

Relationship

Carol is Elaine's first experience of a girl in her own age group. It is soon clear that Elaine finds Carol weak and silly, whereas she views herself as capable, having been raised to be self-sufficient. Elaine often feels isolated from other girls and women, but she also often feels superior to them. Carol reacts to situations emotionally, which Elaine disdains. While Elaine strives to be strong and unaffected, Carol gives into her emotions with enthusiasm.

Key point

Elaine's judgment and inability to identify with Carol show a negative side of the main character: pride and judgment.

Elaine and Stephen Risley (Sister and Brother)

Key quotes

'He thinks he is safe, because he is what he says he is. But he is out in the open, and surrounded by strangers' (p.343).

'He was already moving away from the imprecision of words' (p.3).

Relationship

Stephen is first presented as Elaine's ally. He is imaginative and resilient, and generally a very positive character. As he and Elaine grow older, however, she feels more and more distant from him. She considers asking him for help when Cordelia begins to bully her, but feels he would not know how to make things better. With the strict gender divide enforced at school and socially, she is no longer able to behave in the same way as her brother, yet she is uncomfortable with the silly behaviour of girls like Carol and is at a loss for a third model of behaviour. While she doesn't resent Stephen for his comparable freedom, she feels increasingly disconnected from him and recognises that there is a part of her that wants to find a friend of her own gender to whom she can better relate.

When Elaine and Stephen interact as adults, it is clear they have very different memories of their childhoods, each retaining what is individually relevant and forgetting the rest.

Key point

Stephen is always with Elaine, even after they are no longer close, in the sense that his teenage musings about the nature of time shape Elaine's whole worldview.

Elaine and her mother

Key quotes

'What she wants from me is forgiveness, but for what?' (p.465).

'My mother is not like the other mothers, she doesn't fit in with the idea of them' (p.185).

Relationship

Elaine admires her mother throughout her life. She sees her mother's lifestyle as vastly more appealing than those of her friends' mothers, due to her mother's unconventional attitudes and habits, and admires her for having the confidence to live according to her own preferences. However, when she finds her mother is unable to help her during her difficulties with Cordelia, Elaine's view of her mother shifts slightly.

During this conversation, Elaine's mother says: 'Don't let them push you around. Don't be spineless.' And later in the same scene: 'I wish I knew what to do,' leading Elaine to observe: 'she is powerless' (p.186).

Key point

Elaine's mother is very modern, and her behaviour convinces Elaine it is alright to be different.

Elaine and her father

Key quote

'I want my father to be just my father ... not a separate person with an earlier, mythological life of his own' (p.257).

Relationship

Elaine knows little about her father until later in her life, when she pieces together information about his early life. Like Elaine, he is passionate about what he does for a living. The zoology building, where he works while in Toronto, is a space where her curiosity is rewarded, unlike when she is at school or with her friends. Elaine's father speaks about scientific and social issues to both his children at home, and expects Elaine to behave in a rational manner. The disdain her father shows for anyone he considers irrational or ignorant is reflected in Elaine's distaste for flighty, emotional girls; both she and her father value reason and self-control. However, Elaine's reasoning is that emotion is powerful and dangerous, whereas her father's more pragmatic belief is that reason is an end in and of itself.

Key points

- Elaine enjoys an open dialogue with her father, unlike the relationships her friends have with their fathers.
- Elaine and her father are both very rational but for different reasons.

Elaine and Josef Hrbik

Key quotes

'Josef is rearranging me' (p.358).

'The full weight of Josef rests on me, and he is too heavy for me' (p.377).

Relationship

Josef Hrbik is the Hungarian man who teaches Elaine life drawing at the Toronto College of Art. While she initially finds him glamorous and dramatic, she eventually tires of his ways and leaves him. Josef is presented almost like a test of the self-control Elaine has cultivated; he is romantic and expressive and attempts to get Elaine to react like a 'typical' young woman. Elaine is at first impressed, but in the end she keeps her head and remains unaffected. She is wary of losing control of her emotions with anyone, as the result was so negative when she allowed Cordelia to exert emotional control over her. Josef eventually becomes frustrated, confused as to why he can't produce a more emotional response.

Key points

- Josef introduces Elaine to the art world.
- Elaine's reaction to Josef, contrasted with Susie's, shows how she differs from other women her age.

Elaine and Jon

Key quotes

'What we share, Jon and I, may be a lot like a traffic accident, but we do share it. We are survivors, of each other' (p.18).

'Forgiving men is so much easier than forgiving women' (p.314).

Relationship

Elaine and Jon begin their relationship as friends, meeting in the life drawing class taught by Josef. Jon is first presented as an ally, a figure similar to Elaine's brother Stephen; an honest and upfront male character with whom

Elaine feels a kinship. Jon's straightforwardness is presented in contrast to the secret and shameful world of girls in which Elaine was so miserable. Though Jon's actions during the tumultuous period of their marriage hurt Elaine, she never blames him or resents him, and indeed feels quite tenderly towards him when she visits him while in Toronto for her art show. This is extremely different from Elaine's feeling towards Cordelia.

Key point

Elaine's different reactions to the misdeeds of Cordelia and those of Jon highlight the struggle Elaine has with her feelings towards women and men.

MINOR CHARACTERS

Dr Banerji

Key quote

'He's a creature more like myself: alien and apprehensive' (p.153).

Relationship

Known first as Mr Banerji and later as Dr Banerji (after he successfully earns his PhD from the University of Toronto), this character is an immigrant from India who works with Elaine's father as an entomologist and researcher. Elaine identifies strongly with Dr Banerji, who is an outsider and who is obviously uncomfortable in a new country.

Susie

Key quote

'She is none of the things I've thought about her, she never has been. She's just a nice girl playing dress-ups' (p.375).

Relationship

Susie is another student in the art class taught by Josef. Susie and Josef are already in a relationship when Elaine also begins seeing Josef, presumably without Susie's knowledge. At first Elaine views Susie as manipulative and powerful, a woman who is toying with Josef's emotions. Later she seems weak and obsessed, in Josef's descriptions. But after Susie calls Elaine to her apartment, where Elaine finds Susie unconscious from the botched abortion of Josef's baby, Elaine realises that she and Susie are not very different; that they are both trapped by female standards and roles. Elaine ends up feeling sorry for Susie, but not looking down on her. This is an important process, because Elaine has, up to this point, viewed other women in strict categories, and as creatures very different from herself. Susie is originally presented as a character very similar to Carol Campbell, of whom Elaine was so dismissive. Susie does not fit neatly into any category and Elaine is forced to realise that her binaries may not be absolute.

Sarah and Anne (Elaine's daughters)

Key quote

'They seem to have been born with some kind of protective coating' (p.135).

Relationship

Elaine has two daughters; one with her first husband, Jon, and one with her second husband, Ben. Elaine mentions that she was nervous when she had girls rather than boys. She feared that what happened to her might happen to her daughters, and watched them carefully for signs of this. She is pleasantly surprised, however, to find her daughters extremely resilient. She mentions that she gave them plain, traditional names because Cordelia had a theatrical and unusual name and Elaine wanted to avoid that for her own children (p.15).

Mrs Smeath

Key quote

'Why do I hate [Mrs. Smeath] so much? Why do I care, in any way, what went on in her head?' (p.68).

Relationship

Mrs Smeath becomes the subject of many of Elaine's paintings, despite the fact that it has been many years between Elaine's last interaction with Mrs Smeath and her painting career. Mrs Smeath represents all that is unforgivable in what happened to Elaine. While Cordelia's cruelty stemmed from mimicry of adults and a desire to gain some sense of control in a life where she otherwise had very little, Mrs Smeath's cruelty towards Elaine was motivated by a hatred and fear of anything different from what she was used to. Unlike most families in the area, Elaine's parents were not religious and her mother did not subscribe to a traditional female gender role. Mrs Smeath felt Elaine being punished for her family's oddness was justified, a view Elaine overheard expressed at the Smeaths' house (p.213). Mrs Smeath is someone Elaine can hate in an uncomplicated way, as opposed to Cordelia, for whom her feelings are much more complex.

Ben (Elaine's second husband)

Key quote

'Years before, I would have considered him too obvious, too dull, practically simple-minded' (p.448).

Relationship

Ben, like Sarah and Anne, is never actually heard from in the book, only described by Elaine. This demonstrates that Elaine considers him to be part of her safe, present life. He is presented as a contrast to Jon. As her life goes on, Elaine surrounds herself with people who are less and less like Cordelia; less unstable and less imaginative. While Elaine is clearly happy with Ben, their relationship is a mellower, less intense partnership than any of her past relationships. Ben's main function is to provide comfort and a sense of security for Elaine.

The fathers

Key quote

'In the daily life of houses, fathers are largely invisible' (p.114).

Relationship

The three fathers of Elaine's friends (Grace, Carol and Cordelia) are rarely seen in the book and usually presented as the off-screen disciplinarians of the household. Cordelia is very clearly afraid of her father, and her failed attempts to please him may contribute to her desire to assert control over others. Grace's father is an ineffective, jovial man, who is the only person in the Smeath family with whom Elaine feels any connection – again setting up men as a place of refuge from the harsher world of women. Carol's father is known only as the person who spanks her when she is in serious trouble, such as when the three girls leave Elaine in the frozen river. Elaine feels that her closeness with her father and her brother (the other girls do not have brothers) gives her an advantage over the other girls, while also making her an outsider, a person stuck between the worlds of men and women.

Miranda and Perdita

Key quote

'They are both more charming and beautiful and sophisticated than ever' (p.247).

Relationship

Miranda and Perdita are Cordelia's older sisters. They are adolescents already when Cordelia and Elaine meet, and they tease Cordelia constantly. Their teasing is clearly a model for Cordelia's treatment of Elaine, though it does not seem to be intended in as cruel a manner. Mirrie and Perdie, as they are known, are glamorous and gifted, and seem to please their parents in a way that Cordelia does not. They take quite naturally to their family's upper-middle class social status, whereas Cordelia has trouble deciding where she fits in. Cordelia's uncertainty with her sisters is contrasted with her exquisite control of her peer group.

Miss Stuart

Key quote

'Everyone loves Miss Stuart ... I would love her too, if I had the energy. But I am too numb, too enthralled' (p.184).

Relationship

One of the positive influences in Elaine's young life, Miss Stuart is Elaine's teacher when she is nine years old. She encourages Elaine's early interest in art.

THEMES, IDEAS AND VALUES

Theme #1: Memory and time

Key quotes

'You don't look back along time, but down through it, like water. Sometimes this comes to the surface, sometimes that, sometimes nothing. Nothing goes away' (p.3).

'Time is missing' (p.237).

'I can't remember what I really felt.' (pp.125–26)

Discussion

Throughout the book, Elaine's memories are incomplete and unreliable. She remembers things differently from the other characters, yet her memories are incredibly intense and have a huge impact on her. The divergence becomes apparent when she talks to other characters about her recollections; for example, she discovers that she and her mother remember Elaine's experience of being bullied differently. When talking as teens, it becomes clear that Cordelia remembers their early friendship differently from Elaine, and in a more positive light. As an adult, Elaine's brother Stephen recalls his young life with Elaine differently from her. Sometimes Elaine's memories are more complete than other people's; other times they are incomplete, or missing altogether.

The passage of time is a specific focus of the novel. Elaine observes how Toronto changes, how Canada changes, and is always careful to note the passage of time in concrete ways, such as the death of the King and the resulting changes to Canadian coins. Atwood highlights this theme by having Elaine refer constantly to time in both theoretical and literal ways, and by opening the book with Stephen's observations about the dimension of time. When Elaine gets a job taking Brian Finestein, her next door neighbour's baby son, for walks in his stroller, she mentions that she doesn't know when an hour is up because she doesn't have a watch (p.158). The idea that Elaine is literally unable to perceive time is a clever nod on Atwood's part to the difficulty the character has in keeping the past from affecting her; it is as if no time has passed. In this way, Atwood draws attention to the difference between the literal and emotional perceptions of time, and the instability of those perceptions.

This fluidity of time for Elaine may explain why the deaths of her parents seem somewhat incidental to the storyline. Since her parents are so fully alive in her memories of them from the past, they are in one sense still alive to Elaine, for whom time is not a straightforward experience and for whom the past is as vivid as the present. During her visit to Toronto, when Elaine is an adult, Cordelia is present in Elaine's thoughts to an almost obsessive degree, not always as an adult but often as a young girl. This harkens back to the idea that Elaine's view of time is subjective and influenced more by the impact of an experience than the time period in which it actually took place. In many ways, it seems that what happened to Elaine in Toronto is, on an emotional level, still happening to her. This may be why she seems to resent the changes to the city; the city has moved on, but she isn't able to do the same.

Key points

- Cordelia's hold over Elaine doesn't decrease over time. Time doesn't necessarily diminish the emotional impact of the bullying or other traumatic experiences; in fact, sometimes the negative results are more noticeable later in life.
- Elaine speaks in the present tense for almost the entire book. This shows how, emotionally, she is still trapped in the past:, the past and present are presented in the same way.
- The cat's eye marble becomes a symbol for memory; Elaine remembers things she has repressed when she looks at it as an adult.

Q Are Elaine's memories reliable? How does your answer influence your reading? What is Atwood saying about memory in general?

Q How does time and memory feature in Elaine's artwork?

Q Do you find your memories change over time? Do you remember your childhood in as much detail as Elaine does?

Theme #2: Gender roles and expectations

Key quotes

'[Stephen] has a low opinion of most girls, it seems, and doesn't want me turning into one of the ordinary kind ... a pin-headed fuzzbrain' (p. 258).

'Boys are my secret allies' (p.193).

'I am not normal, I am not like other girls' (p.140).

'I do it, self conscious, as if I'm only doing an imitation of a girl' (p.60).

Discussion

In *Cat's Eye,* Atwood contrasts the physical, male world, with the psychological, female world. Because boys have objective cues to tell them when bullying or violence has gone too far (drawing blood, being knocked down, etc.) the violence is of a different quality than that amongst girls, where limits are more subjective. Elaine also implies that bullying amongst boys is a rite of passage rather than a torment meant to control the victim, contrasting the difference between the bullying Stephen experiences and that conducted by Cordelia: 'after [Stephen's] gone through the fights that are required of any new boy at any school, he's off helping to wage war on the boys from the Catholic school nearby' (p.54).

When the game of marbles becomes popular at school, it is possible that they appeal to Elaine because this is the only activity where boys and girls play together, without the rigid gender separation so common to the era. Part of the reason Cordelia is able to torment Elaine is that she accuses Elaine of not being a normal girl; this is something about which Elaine already feels insecure, and Cordelia exploits that insecurity. When Elaine says 'I am not normal, I am not like other girls' (p.140) she is expressing the widely held belief that the only way to be normal is to conform to expected gender roles – what 'normal' is can change, depending on whether you are a boy or a girl. However, later in life, Elaine sees her difference as a strength. Speaking of the other girls in her university classes, she says: 'I enjoy pestering the girls in this minor, trivial way: it shows I am not like them' (p.334).

When Elaine has children, she mentions that she had originally thought she would have known better what to do with sons than daughters, but the way gender roles have changed since her childhood means she might have been just as unsure with boys. She says: 'But the world of sons has changed; it's more likely to be the boys now with that baffled look' (p.135). This section is important, as it highlights the fact that Atwood is examining gender roles in general, not just the roles imposed on girls.

Key points

- Cordelia is presented as being somewhat in between the world of boys and girls, like Elaine. People who don't fit neatly into a social category can make other people uncomfortable.
- Elaine is judgmental of other girls when they exhibit stereotypical feminine traits, even though she herself is a woman. People are sometimes most unforgiving of traits they are afraid they might also possess.

Q Why does Elaine worry about being different from other girls as a child but later come to enjoy that same difference? What does this say about her emotional needs at different times in her life?

Q Is the pressure that Elaine is facing to behave like a 'normal' girl real or just something she perceives?

Q Are the social expectations for boys and girls still very different? How much have things changed since the era in which Elaine would have been a child?

Theme #3: Belonging and identity

Key quotes

'Whatever is wrong with [Miss Lumley's bloomers] may be wrong with me also ... we line up outside our GIRLS door, whatever category we are in also includes her' (p.95).

'When we bend our heads to pray I feel suffused with goodness, I feel included, taken in' (p.116).

'They are my friends, my girlfriends, my best friends. I have never had any before and I'm terrified of losing them' (p.142).

'But I'm not used to girls, or familiar with their customs. I feel awkward around them, I don't know what to say' (p.54).

Discussion

Throughout her life, Elaine has trouble feeling as though she belongs anywhere. This is true even before she meet Cordelia, which suggests this anxiety is not created by Cordelia, only exploited by her. Elaine feels she belongs in her family, but is aware even as a child that her family is unusual and that eventually she will have to learn to live in a very different kind of world than the one she is used to. Elaine's mother home-schools the children for most of their early education, and Elaine observes a different kind of life in her school reader, saying: 'Nothing in these stories is anything like my life ... These books have an exotic appeal for me' (pp.32–33). Already Elaine perceives a world to which she would like to belong, drawing pictures of what she reads and wishing for a girl friend of her own age.

When Elaine reaches the crisis point in her young life, while she is freezing in the river, she hallucinates an image of the Virgin Mary, who she hears saying: 'You can go home now ... It will be all right. Go home' (p.224). When Elaine is at her most vulnerable, what she wants most desperately is someone to tell her that she is allowed to go somewhere safe, somewhere that she feels a sense of belonging.

Elaine originally feels a sense of belonging with her brother, but soon they are separated both by their diverging interests and by their gender. Elaine describes how, when they were small children, even when she and Stephen fought, they did so quietly and in ways their parents would not notice to avoid getting in trouble. Elaine says: 'Because they're secret, these fights have an extra attraction ... the attraction of conspiracy, of collusion' (p.28). Elaine sees her relationship with her brother as being part of a separate world of children to which adults do not have access. This view that there are separate worlds runs throughout Elaine's childhood, and in fact contributes to her feeling isolated from Stephen once they arrive in the city and the division between boys and girls is more noticeable.

Caught in between the world of girls, where she is told she belongs, and the world of boys, where she is comfortable, Elaine feels trapped once again, as she did when she first entered her house in Toronto. She feels unable to adhere to either gender role when Stephen, Carol and she socialise together. Elaine remembers feeling this conflict and notes: 'So I say nothing' (p.58). Later, she tries to find other ways of belonging, trying to please her friends. She buys treats at the corner store and gives them to the other girls, saying: 'I dole them out equally, these offerings, these atonements, into the waiting hands of my friends. In the moment just before giving, I am loved' (p.160). These offerings are symbolic and represent how, by manipulating Elaine's desire to belong, Cordelia and the others are able to control her.

Belonging is not always a good thing in *Cat's Eye*. Sometimes belonging means giving in to what other people expect, which can be a negative experience in some situations. Elaine realises that she knows how to become a part of the world of girls, but she is unsure if she wants to do what is required. She says: 'Something is unfolding, being revealed to me. I see that there's a whole world of girls and their doings that has been unknown to me, and that I can be part of it without making any effort at all ... All I have to do is sit on the floor and cut frying pans out of the Eaton's Catalogue with embroidery scissors and say I've done it badly. Partly this is a relief' (pp.62–63).

Atwood also uses language to convey Elaine's feeling of isolation. In the first section, when Elaine describes her life with her family in the north, she repeatedly uses the pronouns 'we' and 'ours'. After Elaine's family arrives in the city, the pronoun switches to 'I' and 'mine'.

Key points

- Elaine is both motivated by a desire to belong and afraid of being trapped by the expectations of a group.
- Elaine's need to belong makes her a target for the other girls' bullying.
- Elaine reacts against her need to belong by becoming detached from nearly everyone.

> ***Q*** Does Elaine long for belonging more than other people?
>
> ***Q*** At the end of the novel, has Elaine achieved a sense of belonging?
>
> ***Q*** How does Elaine's home life influence her need for belonging? What about the other girls?

Theme #4: Change and aging

Key quotes

'I have a ferocious desire to be older' (p.241).

'I feel I am older than [my parents], much older. I feel ancient' (p.282).

'For years I wanted to be older, and now I am' (p.309).

Discussion

Part of the theme of aging in *Cat's Eye* is the tension between expectation and reality; the difference between what people hope will happen as they get older and how things actually turn out. Elaine wants to become a successful artist, to escape from Cordelia and to find a supportive partner. She does all of these things, but they don't necessarily fulfill her the way she expected. Even as a child, she finds that getting what she wants doesn't always make her happy, as she discovers when she moves to Toronto: 'At first I found the thought of my own room exciting ... but now I'm lonely' (p.37). Elaine wanted to move to a place where she could find friends, but her first experiences of Toronto are negative and disappointing. This loneliness is symbolic of the isolation she feels throughout her life; the only person she continues to long for as an adult is Cordelia.

When the novel opens, Elaine is middle-aged, and she uses the image of a bridge to describe this point in her life, saying: 'This is the middle of my life. I think of it as a place, like the middle of a river, the middle of a bridge, halfway across, halfway over' (p.13). This is important as a bridge not only features in a very important incident in Elaine's life, but also because a bridge is an in-between location, a place that is neither one side nor the other, reflecting the way Elaine constantly feels: her inability to belong, her difficulties with aging.

Age also has to do with perception. Elaine says: 'The world is being run by people my age, men my age ... it frightens me. When the leaders were older than me I could believe in their wisdom, I could believe they had transcended rage and malice and the need to be loved' (p.311). As a child, Elaine thinks she can outgrow the need to be loved and to belong, but later realises that it is something she will have to deal with for her entire life, and that other people have the same need.

Along with that of aging, the novel addresses the change of choices. The most significant alteration Elaine makes to her life is when she changes social groups, refusing to allow Cordelia and the others to bully her any longer. She says of this choice: 'It's like stepping off a cliff, believing the air will hold you up. And it does' (p.228). Elaine views change as a way of empowering herself because it shows that she can control situations rather than be controlled. That is why aging and changing social trends seem to unnerve Elaine; they are changes over which she has no control. She observes the city of Toronto on her trip, almost obsessively cataloguing the changes that the city has undergone. While observing the city, she says: 'The old emptiness of Toronto is gone. Now it's chock full: Toronto is bloating itself to death, that much is clear' (p.49). She seems to resent the way the city has changed, demonstrating that she mistrusts some of the changes over which she has no control, especially the extreme ones.

Key points

- Aging is a kind of change over which Elaine has no control. This makes her anxious.
- Elaine often takes a long time to make a decision, but once she makes it she is able to affect big changes in her life quite quickly (e.g. leaving her peer group of Cordelia and the other girls, moving to Vancouver).

Q How does Elaine change as she gets older? How does she stay the same? Do people really change as they age or do they just adapt to new situations?

Q What are some expectations Elaine has of adult life? Are her expectations accurate? Does *Cat's Eye* have anything to say about how our expectations can hurt or help us?

Q What other significant changes happen in Elaine's life?

Theme #5: Perception, secrets and knowledge

Key quotes

'What I thought was a secret, something going on among girls, among children, is not one' (p.213).

'I see that I don't have to do what she says and, worse and better, I've never had to do what she says' (p.228).

'I told myself I wanted to see the art; I didn't know I was looking for something' (p.233).

Discussion

In *Cat's Eye* the characters often perceive situations differently than they really are because of their personal experiences or prejudices. Elaine's view of other female characters is influenced by her difficult relationships with girls as a child. For instance, when Susie is in a relationship with Josef, Elaine automatically assumes Susie is the one in control. Later, she is shocked when Susie is left abandoned and injured, saying: 'She is none of the things I've thought about her, she never has been. She's just a nice girl playing dress-ups' (p.375).

Elaine is deeply upset when she realises that her perception of Cordelia's bullying is inaccurate. She assumed that there was a sense of secrecy around her experience, that only she and her so-called friends knew what was happening. However, she realises that Mrs Smeath was aware of the situation, and also that her own mother knew something was going on. She also feels foolish when she realises that she was in fact able to disobey Cordelia, that the only power Cordelia and the others had over her was the power she allowed them to have. There is a significant sense of betrayal when what one perceives is shown to be wrong, because it calls into question whether everything is being perceived inaccurately. Indeed, Atwood seems to question all perceptions when Elaine's memories are shown to be questionable.

The adult Elaine makes a similar point when she discusses her habit of frequenting Catholic churches. She doesn't realise that she is looking for something until she finds a statue of the Virgin Mary that resembles the Virgin Mary of her hallucination in the frozen river. Elaine's perception of her own motivations is unclear to her and when she realises what she was subconsciously looking for, she is deeply moved.

At times it is Elaine herself that questions the accuracy of perception. She feels she is able to bury her emotions, be perceived as happy. She observes a photo and says: 'There I am, in the Grade Six class picture, smiling broadly ... I am as happy as a clam: hard-shelled, firmly closed' (p.237).

Secrets feature largely in Elaine's life. Her biggest secret is the secret of Cordelia's mistreatment of her, but she keeps a variety of large and small secrets, such as her relationship with Josef and the fact that she hears the voice of Cordelia urging her to harm herself at various points in her life. Secrets can be burdensome or positive, depending on how the secret-keeper feels. The secret of Elaine's vision of the Virgin Mary and the secret meaning she has ascribed to her cat's eye marble are both secrets that are very helpful to her, making her feel as though there is a protected part of herself that no one can harm.

Key points

- Elaine often misjudges situations, assuming she knows more than she does about what is happening.
- In *Cat's Eye*, it is shown that there is both danger and power in keeping secrets. Elaine keeps to herself her vision of the Virgin Mary and the significance of her cat's eye marble, and both these secrets are helpful to her. However, she also does not disclose Cordelia's bullying of her, and becomes anxious and ashamed about it.

Q Why does Elaine assume that no one else knows about Cordelia's bullying? What changes for her when she finds out that adults are aware of the situation?

Q Elaine assumes Susie is the dominant one in her relationship with Josef. What causes her to make this assumption? What assumptions does Elaine tend to make about people in general?

Q Are secrets more helpful or harmful? Is keeping a secret always a burden?

DIFFERENT INTREPRETATIONS

Interpreting a text

Different interpretations arise from different responses to a text. Over time, a text will give rise to a wide range of responses from its readers, who may come from various social or cultural groups and live in very different places and historical periods. These responses can be published in newspapers, journals and books by critics and reviewers, or they can be expressed in discussions among readers in the media, classrooms, book groups and so on. While there is no single correct reading or interpretation of a text, it is important to understand that an interpretation is more than a personal opinion – it is the justification of a point of view on the text. To present an interpretation of the text based on your point of view you must use a logical argument and support it with relevant evidence from the text.

The critics' viewpoints

Cat's Eye was well-received on its publication. It was widely reviewed, with *Time* magazine calling it 'a haunting work of art'. Other reviews praised Atwood similarly, saying: 'Irresistible ...This book is about life for all of us' (*The Times*, UK), 'A daring piece of work' (*San Francisco Chronicle*), 'Nightmarish, evocative, heartbreaking' (*The New York Times*).

One of the main subjects reviewers and critics noted was the book's feminist message, or lack thereof. *Publishers Weekly* noted that in Elaine's relationships there existed 'a betrayal of other women that masks a ferocious betrayal of oneself'. Some reviewers felt Atwood was writing a feminist novel in that she was bringing attention to a type of experience women endured that was largely ignored, while others felt she was moving away from traditional feminism and at times even critiquing it by showing how feminism failed to address the harm that women do to one another.

Critics have been interested in whether or not all of Atwood's books should be considered feminist works and whether the author herself should be considered a feminist icon. *The Guardian*, UK, featured a 2009 article quoting Atwood as saying: 'I don't know if I am a feminist.' (Khaleeli, *The Guardian*, 2009) While Atwood has clearly stated that she believes in equality between men and women, she obviously has concerns about the 'feminist' label. Often, debates around feminism are not actually about whether men and women are entitled to the same treatment legally and socially, but rather arguments about what feminism means and how it is perceived. Some people perceive feminism as favouring women over men, while others accept the traditional definition that feminism strives for equality between the genders. Others feel that presenting any kind of gender binary is too limiting. How a particular reader interprets the word 'feminism' is going to influence whether the reader views Atwood's works as feminist.

Interpretation 1

Cat's Eye is a feminist novel, drawing attention to previously neglected issues, in particular that non-physical violence and bullying amongst girls is overlooked and misunderstood.

Jack Illingworth wrote in the official Amazon review of the book, '*Cat's Eye* is a feminist deconstruction of the artist's coming of age novel' (Illingworth, *Amazon.ca*). Many readers might agree that Atwood was using a traditionally feminist framework to look into issues that hadn't been widely examined, such as the development of female artists and the unique non-physical violence practised amongst young girls.

Publishers Weekly noted in its review that '[Atwood's] critical assessment of Cordelia and the "whole world of girls and their doings" also takes the measure of a coercive, conformist society'. This kind of social critique would be a goal of traditional feminist literature. The chance to examine problems of conformity and expectations based on gender in society and to ask questions about those problems would be a traditionally feminist framework for a novel, suggesting *Cat's Eye* could fit into that category.

The book also accomplishes the positive, feminist goal of examining the social development of women apart from romantic relationships, paying attention to women's individual experiences and their treatment of one another. Although the treatment is often negative in *Cat's Eye*, the focus is shifted from the traditional storyline of women's lives being most deeply influenced by men; it instead employs a more modern and feminist story about women affecting each other, showing that women have lives of their own. For instance, Elaine is disappointed with Josef, her first sexual relationship, when she finds he is unable to affect her in nearly as important a way as Cordelia did. When Josef begs her to come back to him, Elaine simply walks away, saying: 'It's like being able to make people appear and vanish at will' (p.378). When compared with Elaine's obsession with Cordelia, from whom she is very much unable to walk away, it is clear who has the deeper effect on the narrator. By paying significant attention to her female characters and showing them to be varied, active and influential, Atwood constructs a traditionally feminist novel.

Interpretation 2

Cat's Eye is not traditionally feminist, and in fact at times critiques the movement, showing how it fails to address the harm done to women by one another.

In an interview for The Reader's Companion to *Cat's Eye* (Atwood, *Cat's Eye*, Doubleday 1998, p.573) Margaret Atwood was asked: 'Do you consider *Cat's Eye* a novel that might advance your reputation as a feminist writer or one that might challenge it?' Atwood answered: 'If by 'feminist' you mean that I write about women – though not exclusively – the answer is yes. *Cat's Eye* is about the underside of little girlhood and about the intricate ways adult women's attitudes evolve from our ambiguous childhood friendships. But if you mean that I see all women as good and all men as bad, then the answer is no. Feminists haven't attacked *Cat's Eye* much; they too were little girls'.

Atwood seems to feel that *Cat's Eye* operates outside a traditional feminist framework, even challenging traditional feminism. It is important to note that just because the author of a text feels one way that does not mean other interpretations are not valid. However, there is support for Atwood's assessment. Jack Illingworth wrote in his review: '[Elaine's] feminism is sceptical and detached ... she has far more sympathy for men than she does for the women who have supported her career' (Illingworth, *Amazon.ca*).

Elaine is a character who is, in some ways, the opposite of a feminist. Rather than holding men and women to equal standards, she is uncomfortable with women and often judgmental of them, while being patient and forgiving with men, even noting to herself: 'Forgiving men is so much easier than forgiving women' (p.314).

Atwood also tackles second-wave feminism head on when Elaine joins a women's discussion group. Elaine states that 'these meetings ... make me nervous' (p.404). She feels that the feminist group, while well-meaning, creates a hostile atmosphere where 'I have no right to speak. I feel as if I'm standing outside a closed door while decisions are being made, disapproving judgments are being pronounced, inside, about me' (p.404). Atwood implies that a traditional feminist framework creates pressure to present women in a positive light at all times, to view men as the source of all social problems. In this sense, a feminist interpretation could limit a reading of the text, implying that Cordelia, as a woman, couldn't be a truly villainous character.

Jack Illingworth puts forward both interpretations in his review, considering the possibilities that *Cat's Eye* is a feminist novel and that it is also a novel that resists such categorisation. In the end, he argues that '*Cat's Eye* transcends orthodox feminism and rigorously examines troubling questions of gender, sexuality, and art from a wryly nonpartisan perspective' (Illingworth, *Amazon.ca*).

QUESTIONS AND ANSWERS

This section focuses on your own analytical writing on the text and gives you strategies for producing high quality responses in your coursework and exam essays.

Essay writing – an overview

An essay is a formal and serious piece of writing that presents your point of view on the text, usually in response to a given essay topic. Your 'point of view' in an essay is your interpretation of the meaning of the text's language, structure, characters, situations and events, supported by detailed analysis of textual evidence.

Analyse – don't summarise

In your essay it is important to avoid simply summarising what happens in a text:

- A **summary** is a description or paraphrase (retelling in different words) of the characters and events. For example: 'Macbeth has a horrifying vision of a dagger dripping with blood before he goes to murder King Duncan'.
- An **analysis** is an explanation of the real meaning or significance that lies 'beneath' the text's words (or images in a film). For example: 'Macbeth's vision of a bloody dagger shows how deeply uneasy he is about the violent act he is contemplating – as well as his sense that supernatural forces are impelling him to act'.

A limited amount of summary is sometimes necessary to let your reader know which part of the text you wish to discuss. However, always keep this to a minimum and follow it immediately with your analysis (explanation) of what this part of the text is really telling us.

Plan your essay

Carefully plan your essay so that you have a clear idea of what you are going to say. A plan will ensure that your ideas flow logically, that your argument remains consistent and that you stay on the topic. An essay plan should be a list of **brief dot points** – no more than half a page. It includes:

- your central argument or main contention – a concise statement (usually in a single sentence) of your overall response to the topic. See 'Analysing a sample topic' for guidelines on how to formulate a main contention.
- three or four dot points for each paragraph indicating the main idea and evidence/examples from the text. Note that in your essay you will need to *expand* on these points and *analyse* the evidence.

Structure your essay

An essay is a complete, self-contained piece of writing. It has a clear beginning (the introduction), middle (several body paragraphs) and end (the last paragraph or conclusion). It should also have a central argument that runs throughout, linking each paragraph to form a coherent whole.

See examples of introductions and conclusions in the 'Analysing a sample topic' and 'Sample answer' sections.

The introduction establishes your overall response to the topic. It includes your main contention and outlines the main evidence you will refer to in the course of the essay. Write your introduction *after* you have done a plan and *before* you write the rest of the essay.

The body paragraphs argue your case – they present evidence from the text and explain how this evidence supports your argument. Each body paragraph needs:

- a strong **topic sentence** (usually the first sentence) that states the main point being made in the paragraph
- **evidence** from the text, including some brief quotations
- **analysis** of the textual evidence explaining its significance and **explanation** of how it supports your argument
- **links back to the topic** in one or more statements, usually towards the end of the paragraph.

Connect the body paragraphs so that your discussion flows smoothly. Use some linking words and phrases like 'similarly' and 'on the other hand', but don't start every paragraph like this. Another strategy is to use a significant word from the last sentence of one paragraph in the first sentence of the next.

Use key terms from the topic – or similes for them – throughout, so the relevance of your discussion to the topic is always clear.

The conclusion ties everything together and finishes the essay. It includes strong statements that emphasise your central argument and provide a clear response to the topic.

Avoid simply restating the points made earlier in the essay – this will end on a very flat note and imply that you have run out of ideas and vocabulary. The conclusion is meant to be a logical extension of what you have written, not just a repetition or summary of it. Writing an effective conclusion can be a challenge. Try using these tips:

- Start by linking back to the final sentence of the second-last paragraph – this helps your writing to 'flow', rather than just leaping back to your main contention straight away.
- Use similes and expressions with equivalent meanings to vary your vocabulary. This allows you to reinforce your line of argument without being repetitive.
- When planning your essay, think of one or two broad statements or observations about the text's wider meaning. These should be related to the topic and your overall argument. Keep them for the conclusion, since they will give you something 'new' to say but still follow logically from your discussion. The introduction will be focused on the topic, but the conclusion can present a wider view of the text.

1 Essay topics

2 What are the different social pressures facing young girls and young boys in *Cat's Eye*?

3 In what sense does the city of Toronto act as a symbol in *Cat's Eye*? What does Toronto mean to Elaine?

4 Elaine becomes an artist and paints subjects from the most vulnerable time in her life. Why does Elaine turn to art and what function does her art serve for her?

5 Cordelia and Elaine seem strongly drawn to each other throughout their lives. Why does this attraction exist? In what ways are they similar? What parallels does the author try to create in their relationship?

6 Elaine constantly sees two 'worlds' – the worlds of children and adults, the worlds of boys and girls. Why does she present things in this way? Are these real or perceived separations?

7 There are fifteen separately titled sections in the novel. What is the significance of the titles chosen in relation to Elaine and her life?

8 Cordelia targets Elaine in a very conscious way. Why does she pick Elaine and what factors contribute to Cordelia's behaviour? What conclusions can be drawn about Cordelia from the information provided by both the child and adult Elaine?

9 The theme of belonging runs strongly throughout the novel. Which characters struggle with a sense of belonging and why? To which characters does belonging not seem to be an issue and why?

10 What is the significance of the cat's eye marble in the novel? Why did Atwood choose to use that for the title?

11 Should *Cat's Eye* be considered a 'feminist' novel? In what ways does it fit that description, and in what ways does it challenge it?

Useful vocabulary for writing about *Cat's Eye*

Feminism: A social movement that believes in and promotes social and legal equality between men and women.

Symbol/symbolic: In literature, a symbol is a physical object used to represent an abstract idea. For instance, you might say that a character's house is symbolic of his or her sense of safety.

Unreliable narrator: This is a term used when a first person point-of-view narrator in a book may not always be telling the truth, either on purpose (lying to the reader) or because the narrator does not have all the information, is mistaken in some way or is unable to tell the truth (due to mental illness, an imperfect memory or other obstacles).

Subjective and objective: Subjective refers to someone's personal viewpoint and means that it is possible for there to be different opinions about something without any one person being proven right. For instance, you might listen to a piece of music and think it sounds very sad. Another person might listen to the same piece of music and think it sounds angry. Neither person is more right than the other because listening to music is a subjective experience; there is no way to prove rationally who is right. If a situation or event is subjective, that means it is a matter of opinion. Objective refers to actual situations or facts, it is impartial and thus the opposite of subjective. It means that there is a right answer in a given situation and the situation is not open to individual interpretations.

Foreshadowing: This is when something happens in a story to hint at or predict something related that will happen later. For instance, in *Cat's Eye*, Elaine and her young friends play doctor only shortly before her mother suffers a miscarriage and has to go to the hospital.

Sample analysis of an essay topic

Topic: *What is the significance of the cat's eye marble in the novel? Why did Atwood choose to use that for the title?*

This topic asks you to look at the marble in the novel as a symbol in Elaine's life and to discover why the marble is so important that Atwood chose to use it for the book's title. Consider the fact that the marble may represent more than one thing to Elaine, because she feels differently about it at different points in the book. It will be helpful to review the sections in which the marble appears prominently, including chapters 12, 27, 38 and 69. Those are the chapters where you will find evidence to back up your points about the significance of the cat's eye marble. Remember to use quotations from the book to support your points.

Read the sample question carefully, and note that it has two parts. The first part asks about the significance of the marble in the book, which may have more than one answer. The second part of the question asks why the marble features in the title and what Atwood might be trying to communicate by choosing that title. What did the title mean to you before you read the book? What about once you had finished reading?

Think about how Elaine's feelings towards the marble change over the course of the novel. At one point, she carries it with her in her pocket, but later she hardly remembers what it is. Still later, it triggers a flood of memories. Why do her feelings change and what does this say about the main themes of the novel? How does Elaine feel about the marble at the end of the novel, and what does that say about the emotional outcome of the story? Does it raise questions about Elaine's reliability as a narrator earlier in the book? Do you trust everything Elaine says?

Introduction

The image of a cat's eye marble appears at several points during the narrative of Margaret Atwood's *Cat's Eye*. The marble offers comfort to the main character, Elaine, representing different concepts at different points in her life. The marble first appears as a neutral space between the worlds of girls and boys. Later it represents the hard, invulnerable and protected qualities which Elaine strives to cultivate, and still later it acts as a container and catalyst for memories. What do these changes in her feelings about the marble represent? How does Elaine's relationship to the marble mirror her relationship with Cordelia?

Body paragraph 1

Main point: The marble appears initially as a neutral space between the world of girls and the world of boys, because marbles are one of the few games played by both. This neutral activity offers relief at a time when Elaine feels uncomfortable being isolated from her brother and other boys.

Support and evidence

- Discuss Elaine's ease in the past when behaving in a typically 'male' way and her discomfort with what is expected of her as a girl.
- Note how other schoolyard games and activities were strictly divided along gender lines (p.53).
- Examine the first presence of marbles at the school, how they give Elaine an excuse to socialise with her brother, and how they bring together boys and girls in a physical space (p.72).

Body paragraph 2

Main point: Next time the marble is discussed, Elaine is suffering the worst of Cordelia's bullying, and she carries it as a protective talisman. At this point, the marble represents what Elaine wants to be, rather than a way of relating (as it did previously). Elaine wants to be hard and strong, like the marble, in order to withstand the mistreatment she receives from Cordelia and the other girls.

Support and evidence

- Show how Elaine keeps the marble with her secretly, and what value secrets have to Elaine (pp.167–68).
- Elaine describes the marble as being 'like something frozen in the ice' (p.167) foreshadowing her own near-freezing experience. What role does hardness and coldness serve in Elaine's emotional life? How does the marble fit, symbolically, into that description?
- Examine Elaine's detachment, socially and emotionally, as she gets older and how this might relate, symbolically, to the marble.

Body paragraph 3

Main point: The final time the marble appears is when Elaine finds it in her parents' house. This is a crucial event in the book, as Elaine, when she looks at the marble, remembers things she has repressed. This is arguably the most important thing the marble symbolises and is the reason Atwood chose the marble for the title: the final role of the marble is to represent a container into which Elaine has stuffed all the unpleasant memories of her childhood. Finding it allows her to remember and deal with everything that happened to her. In this sense, the marble is actively communicating information. Items like this often appear in fiction (for example, a journal or a letter) but the marble is a unique choice as a container for information because it doesn't hold information itself, externally to the narrator. Rather, it unlocks information that the narrator herself holds, internally.

Support and evidence

- Refer to the scene in which Elaine finds the marble to show how it holds, for her, memories of her young life (p.468).
- Examine how, before finding the marble again, Elaine's memories are not always reliable.
- Discuss how this repression of memories has both helped and harmed Elaine over her life.

Conclusion

Atwood uses the cat's eye marble to draw together all of Elaine's different experiences and find meaning in them. It becomes a symbol of what Elaine needs at any given time, offering her comfort, protection and closure when each of those things is called for. Because the marble can only offer what Elaine herself is able to provide, it is also a symbol of her strength and strategy in getting through difficult times, showing the triumph of the narrator through various difficult situations. So while many of the events in *Cat's Eye* are very dark, by choosing a title that hints at redemption, Atwood suggests that she believes people can emerge from such negative situations in a positive way.

SAMPLE ANSWER

Topic: *Cordelia and Elaine seem strongly drawn to each other throughout their lives. Why does this attraction exist? In what ways are they similar? In what ways are they different? What parallels does the author try to create in their relationship?*

Sample answer

As a child, Elaine draws pictures of little girls and longs for a female friend to whom she can relate. She gets her wish in an unexpected and painful way when she meets Cordelia. Though the two girls do not immediately seem similar, they in fact share important traits that make them unique in their peer group and bring about their lifelong attraction to one another.

One of the things Elaine and Cordelia share is a desire to belong and an anxiety that they do not. However, Elaine and Cordelia deal very differently with their inability to fit in. By faking illness and learning how to faint, Elaine becomes detached, revealing her artist's nature as more of an observer than a participant. This detachment becomes more emotional later in life, as Elaine explains, saying: 'I can't believe in my own sadness, I can't take it seriously' (p.245). Elaine no longer needs to faint to separate herself socially, instead she merely resists intense emotional connection, as she does with Josef. While Susie gets swept away, Elaine remains unaffected. Later with Jon, Elaine detaches herself by leaving. Elaine's instinct for self-preservation trumps her need for belonging.

Cordelia, on the other hand, throws herself energetically into her attempt to become part of various groups, even to her own detriment. In this sense, she appears to crave belonging even more than Elaine. Her bullying of Elaine can be interpreted as her first attempt at belonging; when she arrives as the newest member of the group, she overcompensates by positioning herself as the dominant one, ensuring that no one can cast her out. Indeed, none of her cruel actions seem to make her happy, further suggesting she was motivated by a fear of being mistreated herself rather than by sadistic pleasure, as she confirms when she later tells Elaine that she was unhappy throughout those years and considered Elaine her only friend (p.299). Later, Cordelia changes herself constantly, trying to fit in with the other high school students and later still her theatre company, but she never seems content. While Elaine seems to grow to distrust her own need to belong, pulling away from every social group she encounters, Cordelia repeats the same patterns of attempting to fit in until she ends up in a mental hospital. Cordelia represents what Elaine might have developed into if she hadn't decided to become hard and detached, inspired by her cat's eye marble.

The reason Elaine is so strongly attracted to Cordelia despite encountering other characters who share her need to belong (Dr Banerji, for example) is that she and Cordelia are alike in so many other ways. Cordelia is the only girl in Elaine's peer group who shares her rejection of the stereotypical female characteristics of the time. Cordelia is imaginative and active, and in many ways their relationship is very similar to the one Elaine has with her brother Stephen, before Cordelia begins her mistreatment of Elaine. Unlike their other friends, Carol and Grace, Cordelia shares Elaine's creativity and her adventurous spirit, her willingness to explore and get dirty. At their very first meeting, Cordelia is described in terms very similar to Elaine – she is wearing pants while Grace and Carol wear skirts – and she says to Elaine 'There's dog poop on your shoe' (p.83), something Grace and Carol would consider inappropriate to say. Elaine is instantly drawn to her, saying 'She creates a circle of two, takes me in' (p.83). Elaine's longing to belong goes beyond the simple need to be included; she wants to be part of a group of people similar to herself. That desire could have been fulfilled by Cordelia, had things gone differently. Indeed, Elaine praises Cordelia as being similar to herself, saying: 'I divide the people I know into tame and wild. My mother, wild. My father and brother, also wild ... Cordelia, wild, pure and simple' (p.154).

While there are many similar aspects in the characters of Elaine and Cordelia, there is an important difference between the two girls: whereas Elaine has a supportive family, in which she fits comfortably, Cordelia's family treats her as disappointing, laughable and at times even embarrassing. Elaine observes when she visits her that the hospital Cordelia is in is 'the sort of place well-off people use for stowing away those members of their families who are not considered fit to run around in public' (p.416). In this sense, Atwood presents the need to belong as a dangerous impulse that, if left unchecked and compounded by an unsupportive home life, can motivate self-destructive actions. She uses Elaine and Cordelia's lives to illustrate two possible outcomes of this desire and observes how such a need can be managed but never be completely erased: the novel closes with Elaine still longing for a friendship with Cordelia, a relationship of equals in which she could feel that she truly belongs.

REFERENCES AND READING

Atwood, Margaret, 2009, repr. 2011, *Cat's Eye*, Virago Press, London. (First published 1989 by Bloomsbury Publishing.)

Texts about Margaret Atwood

There are many critical and biographical texts about Margaret Atwood and her work. Below is a small sample of works available about Atwood's life and writing.

Cooke, Nathalie 1998, *Margaret Atwood: A Biography*, ECW Press, Toronto.

Cooke, Nathalie 2004, *Margaret Atwood: A Critical Companion*, Greenwood Press, Santa Barbara.

Gale, Stephen H. and Reingard Nischik, eds. 2000, *Margaret Atwood Works & Impact*, Hushion House, Toronto.

Gorjup, Branko 2008, *Margaret Atwood: Essays on Her Work*, Guernica Editions, Toronto.

Illingworth, Jack. 'Amazon.ca review', *Amazon.ca* <http://www.amazon.ca/Cats-Eye-Margaret-Atwood/dp/0770428231/ref=sr_1_1?ie=UTF8&qid=1308579631&sr=8-1>.

Khaleeli, Home. 'Are You a Feminist?' *The Guardian*, 9 September 2009. <http://www.guardian.co.uk/lifeandstyle/2009/sep/09/feminism-margaret-atwood>.

MacPherson, Heidi 2010, *The Cambridge Introduction to Margaret Atwood*, Cambridge University Press, Cambridge.

McWilliams, Ellen 2009, *Margaret Atwood and the Female Bildungsroman*, Ashgate Publishing Company, Surrey.

Sullivan, Rosemary 1998, *The Red Shoes: Margaret Atwood Starting Out*, HarperCollins Canada, Toronto.